P9-CBR-986

This is a story about people. People who
obeyed God and got blessed; people who disobeyed
God and got wrapped soundly on the knuckles.
Some of them learned, some of them refused to
learn. But they all had one thing in common and
it was this: Somewhere, somehow, GOD stepped
into each of their lives. At just the right time.
And in just the right way. And when *He* stepped in,
the strangest things began to happen . . .

**Other Regal Venture
Books by Ethel Barrett**

These Regal Venture books make Bible stories
come-alive for readers of every age. Also
provide exciting resources for G/L pre-teens
Bible studies.

For Family Bible storytimes

"The strangest thing happened...

BY ETHEL BARRETT

A Regal Venture Book
A Division of G/L Publications
Glendale, California, U.S.A.

Over 300,000 in print
Second printing, 1970
Third printing, 1970
Fourth printing, 1971
Fifth printing, 1972
Sixth printing, 1974
Seventh printing, 1975
Eighth printing, 1976
Ninth printing, 1978

Published by
Regal Books Division, G/L Publications
Glendale, California 91209
Printed in U.S.A.

Library of Congress Catalog Card No. 76-84599
ISBN 0-8307-0005-6

Contents

A teaching and discussion guide for use with this book is available from your church supplier.

CHAPTER 1

The Kingdom
that Fell Apart

This book is a story of a kingdom that came apart at the seams. And the name of the kingdom was Israel. It's a thundering story of kings and prophets and wars and spies and ambush and trickery—of bravery and cowardice—of shining honesty and outrageous mischief—and a few things more.

Actually, though, when you get right down to it, it's a story of *people*. People who obeyed God and got blessed; people who disobeyed God and got rapped soundly on the knuckles. Some of them learned, some of them refused to learn. But they all had one thing in common and it was this: Somewhere, somehow, GOD stepped into each of their lives. At just the right time. And in just the right way. And when *He* stepped in, the *strangest things began to happen!*

How It All Began

It began with the man who had everything. His name was Solomon, and well you know him, for he was one of the most blazing characters in history. He was a man whose glory and greatness started with a dream. He might have been an ordinary king except for that dream. No one has ever had a dream like it before or since.

2

"Ask me," said God in the dream, "and I'll give you anything you desire." Anything? *Anything?* Riches? Long life? Happiness? The list of things that come to your mind!

But Solomon made a most amazing request. He asked for *wisdom* to rule his people. And from that moment he stopped being ordinary and zoomed into greatness.

"Because you have asked for wisdom," said God, "and not long life or riches or the life of your enemies, I'll *give* you a wise and understanding heart. And I'll also give you riches and honor so there will be none like you in all the world." And God kept His promise, so much so that there is hardly a person alive who has not heard of the wisdom of Solomon. There was no subject under the sun he did not know about. And riches! Beyond belief! And Solomon began to build.

The Kingdom that Had Everything

There was absolutely no counting the wealth in Solomon's kingdom; it went up into the impossibidrillions. The palaces he built, the roads, the pools, the stables, the cities —and the magnificent Temple for God in Jerusalem! Israel was the talk of the civilized world!

It was after the Temple was built that God appeared again to Solomon in a dream (I Kings 9:1-7) and issued a solemn warning. "If you follow me and keep my laws, I will bless you," said God, "BUT. If you go after other gods. . . ." (Read it in verse 7. God was saying, in effect, *"Watch it!* The Temple will come down and the country will come apart!")

Solomon built on. And on. A fleet of ships, ivory and gold thrones, chariots, shields of gold, more palaces—on and on.

But he forgot to "watch it." It was a fair enough warning but he did not heed it.

Down We Go

Solomon began to flirt with idol-worshiping countries. He made treaties *with* them. And he married wives *from* them. This was a deadly combination. The people from these countries began to trickle into Israel to live. Solomon built palaces for his wives, and temples and altars for the people so they could worship their own gods. Between the treaties and the wives, the palaces and temples sprang up like mushrooms.

Now you can see at once that this was going to lead to nothing but trouble, which it did. For Solomon had what the Bible calls "largeness of heart," which means that he had such an open mind and tried so hard to be cooperative that he began to worship these heathen gods *himself*.

Going . . .

God did not let Solomon dabble in disobedience for long. He had already warned him. Now He *told* him. And the news wasn't good. You can read it in I Kings 11:11-13. After Solomon's death, his kingdom would be divided. Solomon's son Rehoboam would get one piece; someone else would get the rest. The jig was up.

Going . . .

Someone else would get a piece of Israel? Who? *Who?* Solomon began to look upon everyone with suspicion. Almost anyone could be his enemy. For behind the scenes in his magnificent kingdom were angry people. Thirty thousand men of Israel had to spend one out of every three months on building projects! Their burden was heavy and they were furious. Solomon looked for anyone among them who might be a threat. Now when you're looking for trouble you can usually find it. And Solomon was. And he did.

There was a fellow by the name of Jeroboam, in charge of the work force of the tribe of Ephraim. Solomon himself had put him there because he felt that Jeroboam was capable and courageous, a good man. But now that Solomon was suspicious and afraid, Jeroboam looked *too* good. In fact he looked so good that Solomon tried to kill him. Now when you know that someone is trying to kill you (especially a king) you don't wait around for it to happen. You *run*. And Jeroboam did—to Egypt. (Keep your eye on this chap. He'll turn up again.)

Anyhow, Solomon spent his last days in suspicion and fear.

. . . Gone

. . . and then he died. What a magnificent beginning. And what a *miserable* ending. Solomon died, still disobedient to God. We know that God still loved Solomon. But there is not one clue in the Bible that Solomon was ever sorry for the foolish things he had done.

And This Is How It Went

This is when his son Rehoboam stepped into the drama. And this is when the kingdom began to fall apart. And this is how it happened.

Rehoboam was anointed king in Jerusalem. And that should have been the end of it. But it wasn't. For only the people in *Judah* shouted, "Long live the king!" The rest of the enormous kingdom was ominously silent. Look at the map and you'll get the picture.

Now Rehoboam was not about to take this lying down. He took his father's advisors and a group of his own young friends and went up to Shechem to see what was the matter. And when he met with the leaders of the rest of the kingdom, who should their spokesman be but—Jeroboam, fresh back from Egypt! (We *told* you he'd turn up.)

"We'll serve you as king," said Jeroboam, "IF. If you lighten our burden. Stop taking our men one month out of three. Slow down this hysterical building program. And we'll serve you forever."

Rehoboam was so taken back he could only sputter. "Give me three days," he said, "and I'll give you my answer."

Three Days that Changed History

Rehoboam went to his father's advisors. "Grant their request," they said. "Treat them with respect, and the entire kingdom will be yours."

Now Rehoboam should have quit while he was ahead. But he didn't. He went to his friends, his own age, and asked *them* what to do. "Don't let anybody dictate to you!" they cried. "Tell them you are more powerful than your father ever was. Tell them you'll *increase* their burdens. Let them know who's boss!"

So Rehoboam had two choices. And he made the wrong one. He went back to the leaders. And he opened his mouth. And he put his foot in it. He told them what his young friends had said. He told them *he* was the boss. And to prove he wasn't bluffing, he sent a man out into the field to see that the construction crews *did* work harder. It was his first big blast of authority. And his last. For the man he sent out was promptly killed.

Rehoboam's young advisors had steered him right into near disaster. He hopped into his chariot and went back to Jerusalem to sulk.

The Moment of Truth

It was while he was back in Jerusalem that the horrible news came. The people of the northern part of the kingdom had proclaimed Jeroboam king! Monstrous!

"Fight!" bellowed Rehoboam, "We'll fight!" And he called together what army he could muster and prepared to attack. But God was still running this little drama. And before they could get ready to march, a prophet of God came to Rehoboam.

"Thus saith the LORD," said the prophet. "You shall NOT go up nor fight against your brothers. Return to your homes. This thing is from ME." (See I Kings 12:24.)

So Rehoboam did the first smart thing he had done to date. He sent his soldiers home. He accepted his punishment from God. And he sat down to count the cost. He had this much of the kingdom left.

And Jeroboam had all the rest!

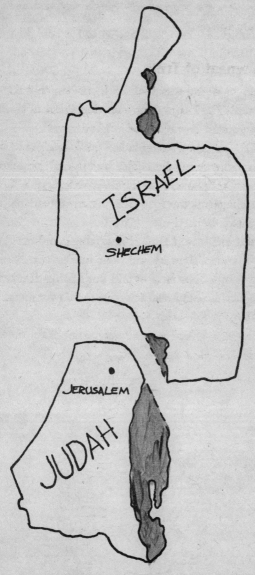

What's It to You?

The most terrific privilege God has given you is the power of choice. He has told you what He has done about your sin (I Corinthians 15:3). And what you can choose to do about it (John 1:12). And He has told you how to live it out: "I have chosen the way of truth" (Psalm 119:30). You may not be a king, but in your own world and in your own life and in your own way, you have the same choices. And sometimes the results of your choices go on and *on*.

Solomon made the wrong choice by turning to the gods of his many wives. Rehoboam made the wrong choice by turning to the chaps his own age for advice instead of to the older more experienced men. And the results of these two choices went on . . . and on . . . and on . . . and on . . . and on. . . .

And the people who step in and out of this drama make the most colorful cast of characters you will ever meet.

CHAPTER 2

"Follow
the Leader"

I Kings 12:25-33; 13:1-6,33,34
II Chronicles 11:13-17

The Smart One

Jeroboam—risen from the ranks, to rule the biggest part
of the divided kingdom. Jeroboam—king of Israel.

What a hero! How adventurous! He'd fled from the wrath
of Solomon, to Egypt, and had barely escaped with his life.
How glamorous! While in Egypt, he'd married no less than
the *Pharaoh's* daughter (a crafty thing to do). But what a
dashing king he made! The people adored him.

And he knew it.

Now popularity is pretty heady business. And it takes a strong person to accept it, thank God for it, use it wisely—and not lose his head over it.

Of course Jeroboam deserved his popularity; he'd worked hard for it. And he was ruling his people wisely and well. Their building program was going splendidly—fortifications at the capital city of Shechem, and at the important city of Penuel—yes, the new kingdom was off to a good start. The people were prosperous and happy. They were worshiping God. They'd be celebrating the Feast of Tabernacles in the fall—

All the wheels in Jeroboam's head ground to a halt.

Feast of Tabernacles! Where would they go to celebrate it? Why to Solomon's Temple—of course. And where was Solomon's Temple? In Jerusalem. And where was Jerusalem? In Judah—Rehoboam's kingdom!

Oh, good grief.

Jeroboam pictured his people streaming into Judah—thousands upon thousands of them. What if they got sentimental about Judah? Or worse still, what if they got sentimental about Rehoboam? What if their hearts and their loyalty turned back to him again? Jeroboam saw his newly-acquired popularity and glory and power go down the drain. He had to think of something. But what? He called his advisors together to see what could be done.

The Man Who Outsmarted Himself

Now you'd think that anyone who "had it made," as Jeroboam did, would have the sense to keep it that way. But Jeroboam, alas, outsmarted himself. The way to keep the people at home, he and his advisors reasoned, was to offer them something to *worship* at home. It would have to be attractive. Something they could *see*. Something—

Why of course! Idols! What else?

Golden calves! Two of them! And one at each end of the kingdom, no less, so nobody would have to travel very far. That would settle everything very nicely. Everyone would be satisfied, Jeroboam would keep his kingdom to himself— and no harm done.

If it seems unbelievable that Jeroboam would do such a thing—it *is*—but he did. And oh, how clever he was about it. "It's too much for you," he said, and his voice was oily, "to go so far to celebrate the Feast of Tabernacles. See—here are your gods, who brought you up out of Egypt. You can worship God at their feet as well as anywhere else."

Now inasmuch as God had specifically told the people that they could celebrate this feast only *at* the Temple, and bring their sacrifices only *to* the Temple, to say nothing of the fact that they were not to worship idols, Jeroboam was slightly amiss on several points.

He Got Smarter and Smarter

One of the most heartbreaking tragedies of doing something wrong is, once you get started you often don't know when to stop. Jeroboam's clever ideas didn't stop with the golden calves. He appointed priests to serve at the altars of these golden calves, and the priests were—just anybody! The Bible says he appointed priests from the "lowest of the people." This might sound nice and democratic, but the fact was that God had commanded Moses that only those in the tribe of Levi could perform the duties of the Temple. And only the Levites who were descendants of Aaron could be priests!

Then he set the date for the celebration—the fifteenth day of the eighth month. Which seems like a reasonable privilege of a king, but the fact was that God had set that date as the fifteenth day of the *seventh* month, for it was a harvest feast of thanksgiving—and it was a holy day, never to be changed.

So by the time the celebration date came, Jeroboam had made shim-shams of God's order of priesthood, had changed the holy day of celebration, had discouraged the people from going to Jerusalem, and had made two golden calves for them to worship. Which is a long low way to go to keep your popularity.

Dan was the city in the north that Jeroboam chose for one of the golden calves. He sent his self-appointed "priests" there, and the people flocked to the celebration like sheep. They were completely hoodwinked. Had not their dashing leader spoken?

Bethel was the city in the south. And Jeroboam chose to go there himself to the celebration. Bethel seemed like a reasonable selection for it was on a main route, and very handy to get to. But Bethel was also the place where Abraham stopped on his way to Shechem and offered a sacrifice.* And where Jacob stopped for the night when he was fleeing from Esau—and where the ladder and the angels descended to him and God spoke to him.** Bethel was one of

* Genesis 12:8; 13:3.
** Genesis 28:10-22.

the holiest places in Israel. Bethel was dear to the heart of God. Jeroboam had sunk pretty low.

The Big Showdown

The celebration began. The people were there at Bethel —great crowds of them, playing "follow the leader" for all the world as if they were children with no minds of their own.

Jeroboam stood by the altar to burn incense. The people looked at him, standing there—this great and charming leader, this breaker of rules, this law-unto-himself—and they thought they were certainly being modern and intelligent and going along with the times.

And then one man stepped out of the crowd. He was a prophet of God. And he stopped the celebration in its tracks. He walked right up to the altar and cried, "Oh, altar, altar!"

The people stared, silent. Jeroboam stared too. They were stunned as the prophet went on to tell them of God's disapproval—that nothing but disaster could come of this nonsense. And no one interrupted. And no one moved. It was as if someone had stopped a home-movie film and frozen the characters in their places.

"And this is the sign that this message is from the Lord," the prophet cried when he had finished, "this altar shall split and the ashes that are on it shall be poured out."

By now Jeroboam had recovered his old spirit. He'd had enough. He leapt into action as if the film had been turned on again. "Lay hold of this man," he bellowed, pointing to the prophet.

17

And then he stopped. And stared at his hand. It was shriveling and drying up before his very eyes! And at the same moment the altar split and the ashes poured out from it, onto the ground!

Now, clearly, *God* had had enough.

There was a stunning silence as they all watched.

"Please—please. Pray for me," Jeroboam said to the prophet at last. "So that my hand will be healed and I can use it again."

The prophet prayed. And as they watched, the miracle happened again in reverse. The hand turned back to normal before their eyes!

Silence. It was such an astonishing exhibition of God's power that for a moment no one could speak. Then Jeroboam recovered himself. He looked back at the prophet. "Come home with me," he said, "and refresh yourself and I'll give you a reward."

And the prophet said, "I would not stay in your house if you *gave* me half of it." And he turned on his heel and left.

Jeroboam looked at the altar, split and crumpled, the ashes spilt out. The crowd broke up, mumbling. The celebration was over.

It had been quite a day.

And TOO Smart, at Last

In spite of this solemn warning, Jeroboam continued to worship his handmade idols with his handpicked priests. He ruled his kingdom in fine style. But some of the power and greatness had gone out of him. He was an empty king now, a bag of wind. For a person who tears up the rule book and makes his own rules can't win for losing. He's wrong even when he's right.

To Follow or Not to Follow?

Most of the people followed him blindly into sin. Most of them. But not all of them. There were a few who "set their hearts to seek the LORD God of Israel." And with no wishy-washy halfway nonsense. They *set their hearts*. This means with grit and determination. So some of them followed and some of them did not. Some of them went on to—but that comes later in our story.

The Big Shot—And Is He Really?

What a hero! How adventurous! How dashing! And what a total disaster. Popularity is pretty heady business. It takes a strong person not to lose his head over it. And it takes a strong person not to "follow the leader" when the leader, no matter how dashing, is going in the wrong direction.

What's It to You?

Are you considered a leader? How much does your popularity mean to you? To what lengths would you go to keep it? What do you think about tearing up the rule book and making up your own rules, when *your* rules are going to make everything more convenient for everybody—but the chances are that they *might* leave everything in a mess?

Are you a follower? If a leader is dashing and successful, how can you tell if he's right?

Supposing a popular leader drops out of your church group and collects a group of his own followers? And it would be more convenient and more exciting to hang around with them? What would you do? How would you arrive at your decision?

Do you know what popularity is? It's "the favor of the public in general or a particular group of people."

How far would *you* go to be popular? Is it worth it?

A good verse to guide you is, "Hear, O Israel: The LORD our God is one LORD: And thou shalt love the LORD thy God with all thine heart, and with all thy soul, and with all thy might" (Deuteronomy 6:4,5).

CHAPTER 3

How to Be
Ten Feet Tall

The Little Man Who Almost Wasn't There

Rehoboam—son and rightful heir of King Solomon, left with half of the divided kingdom—and the smaller half at that.

What a failure. How embarrassing. He'd fled from Israel in disgrace. How stupid. He'd asked the young men his own age for counsel, decided to be a smart aleck, and lost more than half his crown to Jeroboam.

What a wretched business.

It was a dismal start for his reign. But he picked himself up and decided to make the best of it.

The Best of a Bad Deal

Actually, his achievements were rather remarkable. In a flurry of activity, he set about to make his little kingdom strong enough to defend itself.

Fortify the cities! Every important city all over Judah was fortified—in the hill country, the coastal plains, along the Dead Sea, in the wilderness.

Train the men! He sent army commanders to train the men and get them ready for possible warfare. Give them weapons! He sent shields and spears for the men to use. Be ready for siege! He filled storage houses with food and oil and wine so they'd have spare food for months in case of attack. Keep the program humming! He sent one of his most capable sons to each city to manage the operations and see that things did not lag.

In addition to all the physical things he was doing to make his nation strong, spiritual strength was pouring into his country with no effort on his part at all. Yes. Godly people were coming across his borders from the kingdom of Israel. Refugees. The priests and Levites Jeroboam had snubbed—and people who had "set their hearts to seek the LORD God of Israel." Rehoboam, as the saying goes, never had it so good. And this went on for three wonderful years.

Comfort, Comfort, Thy Name CAN Spell Trouble

It was after all these things were done that Rehoboam felt he could relax and be comfortable. So he relaxed. And got comfortable. *Too* comfortable. In fact he got more than comfortable. He got careless. And he neglected his worship of God. And so did his people.

Then some of his people sneaked off to the hills, set up altars and idols, and went to it with idol worship again, and he looked the other way. Then more of them. And more of them. Until, the Bible says, "Rehoboam . . . forsook the law of the Lord, and all Israel with him" (II Chronicles 12:1, Amplified*). It's exactly what they did, and what's more, they got away with it. They got away with it for two years. And then everything exploded.

Red Alert!

It came with shattering suddenness, and hit like buckshot, scattering in every direction. Shishak, the pharaoh of Egypt had invaded Judah! Messengers came stumbling into the palace to confront a stunned Rehoboam with bulletins, late bulletins and late-late bulletins. The fortified cities were falling! Mareshah—Etam—Tekoa—

Shishak's mighty army had a battalion of more than a thousand chariots! Ziph—Hebron—Lachish—Beth-zur—

Hundreds of thousands of soldiers, pouring in, conquering! Rehoboam's sons coming back to Jerusalem to report that they'd barely escaped with their lives as their city fell! Gath—Bethlehem—Adullam—Zorah—

City after city after city. And then—Shishak began marching toward Jerusalem itself! And in this darkest hour, who should come on the scene but a man of God named Shemaiah—and what should he say but that God had aban-

* From "The Amplified Bible." Used by permission of Zondervan Publishing House, Grand Rapids, Michigan.

doned Rehoboam! "Thus says the Lord, You have forsaken Me, so I have abandoned you to the hand of Shishak"*

The Name of the Game Is Choice

For the second time in his career, Rehoboam had a choice to make that would shiver the timbers of his kingdom. This time he did it right. He *humbled* himself. "The Lord is righteous,"** he said simply. No quibbling. No blaming anyone else. No "But I inherited this mess from my father, Solomon!" No "I was too busy with all my activities to have time for worship!" And no whining. He had a choice and he decided to come clean and admit he was dead wrong. It was in this moment of complete honesty and humility that he stopped being a little man and became ten feet tall. And it was at this moment that God changed His mind and lessened the punishment.

* II Chronicles 12:5, Amplified.

** This means the Lord is **right,** and no nonsense.

26

"They have humbled themselves," said God, "so I will not let Shishak destroy them—"

It's Still Going to Hurt a Little

"—BUT."

God forgave Rehoboam, but he didn't get off scot-free. In some peculiar way his punishment turned out to be that he got exactly what he had wanted. He had wanted to get out from under God's law.

"—so I will not let Shishak destroy them," God said, "BUT. Inasmuch as they did not want to be *My* servants— I'll let them be *Shishak's* servants. And let them find out the difference!"

The difference was pretty humiliating business. Rehoboam couldn't fight Shishak. He didn't dare. It would have taken a miracle of God to win, and God had promised no such thing. The only thing left for Rehoboam to do was to pick up the pieces he'd smashed and try to make the best of what was left. He asked Shishak for terms of surrender.

And they hurt.

Shishak took all the treasures that had been stored in the Temple and in the palace. All the booty. All the gifts David had got from all the countries between Assyria and Egypt. And all the golden shields that Solomon had made. Two hundred large shields and three hundred smaller ones made of pure gold and stored in the guardroom of the palace.

It hurt, it hurt.

Rehoboam had fallen away from God. Rehoboam had repented. Things weren't as good as they might have been.

But they were better than they would have been if Rehoboam had not repented.

Better than total disaster.

What's It to You?

1. You don't have to dash off and worship idols to find yourself in the same boat Rehoboam was. He got so comfortable he forgot God. But the big lesson in his story is that he was willing to admit he was wrong, and take the consequences. Do you think he should have had to take the consequences after he repented? Why do you think God made him do so?

2. Jan borrowed her brother's bike. She neglected one little formality; she forgot to ask him for it. She would have got by very nicely too, except for a careless driver who made an unexpected turn and—zoom, into a pole she went to avoid the oncoming car. And the bike? Color it well-crumpled.

   Jan has several ways to go. Can you think of some of them? Some of them involve the old buck-passing; one of them is downright sneaky.

3. If someone in your group owned up to something he had done, would you think he was ten feet tall or a dum-dum? If you owned up to something would you expect to escape the consequences?

4. Memorize: "Draw nigh to God, and he will draw nigh to you. Cleanse your hands, ye sinners; and purify your hearts, ye double minded. Humble yourselves in the sight of the Lord, and he shall lift you up" (James 4:8,10).

CHAPTER 4

Why Did You Have to Go and Spoil It All?

II Chronicles 14:1–16:14

Off to a Smashing Start

"Long live the king!"

A young man he was, standing there before the crowds.

"Long live the king!"

His grandfather had been King Rehoboam, and a rocky time *he'd* had of it—he'd gone down in history as a weak king. The young man waved to the cheering people.

"Long live the king!"

His father had been Rehoboam's son Abijah, and a good king he'd been, walking before the Lord—but he'd reigned only three years and now he was dead and the young man was suddenly in power.

"Long live King Asa!"

Asa was the young man's name. He had a big job cut out for him. And he meant to do it well.

A "Cleanup Week" that Lasted Ten Years

The Bible says, "And Asa did what was good and right in the eyes of the Lord his God" (II Chronicles 14:2, Amplified). Now you can be "good and right" by just staying home and doing nothing. Asa wasn't this sort of a king. He did what was good with a vengeance.

He went over Judah's defense program like a five-star general. Better cities! Build them up! Higher walls! Stronger gates and bars! While we have peace, don't drag your feet! Better trained army! Never be caught with too little too late! Get going!

And he went over Judah's worship program like a new broom. High places with altars? Out. Idols? Out, *out*. For he realized that their tiny country could never survive against her powerful neighbors except by the grace of God. Idols were *out*. God was *in*.

These were golden days in Judah. How simple everything was, trusting the Lord completely, how uncluttered and good.

Things Get Better—

Even when the news came that the army of Ethiopia was advancing toward Judah from the south, there was no panic in Judah. Asa marched his well-trained, well-equipped army out against the enemy—three hundred battalions armed with spears and shields, 280 battalions in gleaming armor, bearing bows and arrows. But his faith was not in his army. His faith was in God.

Good thing, too.

Whatever Asa's army had, the Ethiopian army had twice as much, plus a huge chariot force. Judah's army was dwarfed by the comparison!

Asa just believed God.

"Lord, it is nothing to you to give victory to an army, whether it is large or small. So help us, O Lord our God; we are trusting You, and we go to meet that tremendous army in Your name."*

And he followed up his words with action and ordered his army forward. And the Lord heard his prayer and Judah won—Judah won every battle where that war was fought and captured every city connected with each battle. And came home with booty beyond belief—gold and silver and treasures and sheep and oxen and camels. Beyond counting, all of it.

And Better—

When they returned to Jerusalem with all this booty, a prophet of God came out to meet them. "Hear me, Asa, and all the rest of you," he cried. They listened respectfully. "The Lord is with you," he went on, *while you are with Him. If you seek Him, He will be found. But—*" And here was the solemn part—"if you forsake *Him,* He will forsake *you.*" Then he gave them a rundown on some of the history

* See II Chronicles 14:11.

of Judah to remind them that these were not idle words. It had *always* happened that way. They were silent and respectful. "So be strong!" he concluded, "And don't let your hands be weak—for your work shall be rewarded!"

And BETTER—

They drank in every word. And brought their booty home. And poured into Jerusalem and held a tremendous thanksgiving service to God. What a celebration it was! Singing and shouting and trumpets and horns! And promises! They promised God they would follow Him with all their hearts.

Then they stashed their treasures in the Temple storeroom and settled down to peace once more.

This Time It's for Real

The golden days ran into golden years. There was peace and prosperity all over Judah. Five years—ten years—twenty years—twenty-five years—

Twenty-five trouble free years—believing God and worshiping Him and depending on Him. How wonderful. There was no doubt about it, it was the only way to go.

So naturally, when Israel got mischievous again and everything started coming up trouble, Asa knew just where to turn. He turned to the king of Syria—

What?

The king of Syria? King Ben-hadad? In Damascus? King of *Syria*?

Why?

Did Asa panic? Did he forget? We don't know. It was the mystery of the century. In one fell-swoop, Asa threw thirty-five golden years down the drain, and picked up the bill for a package of grief.

"Please, God—I'd Rather Do It Myself"

There's no doubt about it, Asa's problem was a real one. King Baasha of Israel had the *nerve* to lead his army *clear into Judah,* right up to the city of Ramah, and proceed to build a fort. From there he blocked the main highway into Jerusalem and intercepted everyone coming from and going into that important city. Now this was as bad as a full-scale invasion and of course *had* to be squashed.

And there's no doubt about it, Asa's strategy was clever. He took the treasures out of the Temple storeroom and out of the palace and sent them to King Ben-hadad of Syria with a message: "Let's make a treaty. All this treasure is yours if you'll break your treaty with King Baasha of Israel and make him pull out of Judah."

It was a bribe. And a sneaky one at that. And King Ben-hadad accepted it. And he got Baasha out of Judah in a very roundabout way. He sneaked over into the *north of Israel* and began attacking important cities there. When King Baasha got wind of it, way down south in Judah, he packed up his troops, pulled out of Judah, and made for home to defend his own cities, leaving his timber behind him.

Clever!

That left Asa free to tear down the fort Ben-hadad was

building at Ramah, carry off the timber and stones and build two *new* fortified cities.

Jolly!

The Payoff

No, not so jolly. For a man of God came to Asa again, and this time the news was not good. "You have relied on the king of Syria and not on God," he roared, and, "Weren't the Ethiopians a bigger army and didn't the Lord give you victory over them?" And he concluded sadly, "You have done foolishly; for this, you shall have wars."

The golden days were over.

The Name of the Game Is Choice

Here it is again. Choice. Rehoboam had had the same choice when he'd been rapped on the knuckles. And he'd said, "The Lord is righteous." And he had repented.

But Asa got angry.

He got angry and had the man of God chained in prison.

The End of the Game Is Auuuugh

It was a sad ending to a wonderful tale of daring-do and golden years of peace and prosperity. From the moment Asa got angry and refused to take his knuckle-rapping in the right spirit, he began to run down like a wooden clock. Even when he was stricken with disease in his old age, he refused to turn to God. And he wound up angry and bitter, like an old buck tangled in his own horns, and died without repenting.

What a pity. God didn't forget or overlook all the good years, though. For most of Asa's life *was* great. And he went down in history as a good king.

But what a shame to have to write such a sad ending to such a great story!

What's It to You?

1. Does it seem to you ridiculous that Asa could have taken such a nose dive after he'd been such a great person all those years? Do you suspect that God might be saying, "Watch it!" to you through this story?

2. Memorize this verse and think about it. "Wherefore let him that thinketh he standeth take heed lest he fall" (I Corinthians 10:12).

3. What do you think makes people forget God's goodness like that? Can you think of times in your life that you have forgotten and fallen right on your face? Don't you feel silly?

CHAPTER 5

The Prophet Who Went Out on a Limb

Meanwhile, Back in Israel—

What was going on in Israel during these fifty years? Trouble aplenty. After Jeroboam's (remember him?) miserable reign, the kings rose and fell like pop-ups; the players came and went in such confusion during these years, you couldn't tell who they were without a program.

First, Jeroboam's son Nadab. He ruled two years and was killed in a revolt, led by a man named Baasha. Next king— Baasha. His rule? Full of invasions, wars and trouble. Then *his* son Elah, who was killed by Zimri. Next king? Zimri, naturally. But when the army got wind of Elah's murder, they pounced on Zimri, who promptly went to the palace and killed himself. He had ruled for seven days! Next king?

Commander of the army—Omri. Next king? Omri's son Ahab. If this seems confusing to you, think how confusing it was to them; you only have to study it—they had to *live* through it.

So now, while King Asa was threshing about in the last few years of his reign in Judah, it was fifty years, six kings and many battles later in Israel. And the news was not good.

The Worst Husband-Wife Team in History

Being famous can be good or bad, depending on what you're famous for. Ahab had the doubtful distinction of being the worst king Israel had ever had. Now Ahab could have been quite wicked enough by himself without any help, but he had married a woman quite as bad as he—or worse. She was a Phoenician princess. She had a fierce domineering nature. She stirred him up to evil, the Bible says. She worshiped idols. And she absolutely hated God. Her god was Baal, and when she became queen, she was determined that everyone else was going to worship Baal too. Her name was Jezebel. Now you can see, with this combination, things are going to get worse.

God Said "ENOUGH!"

Ahab went along with this nonsense as if he'd had a ring in his nose. He built a temple for Baal, hired hundreds of *priests* for Baal, and made the *worship* of Baal the national religion! Prophets of God were killed wholesale, and the people who still believed in God did not dare say so. It was

at this point that God stepped in. It was as if God were saying, *"Enough!"* The bad news came like a bombshell. And
through an unexpected visitor.

The Prophet Who Went Out on a Limb

His name was Elijah and nobody could stop him! Nobody
tried to. They were too astonished to do anything but stare.
He strode past the guards, up to the throne, and without
any preliminaries, looked Ahab in the eye and said, "As the
LORD God of Israel liveth, before whom I stand, there
shall not be dew nor rain these years, but according to my
word" (I Kings 17:1). There was a shocked silence; nobody
could quite believe what he had heard. Then Elijah turned
on his heel and strode past the guards, into the court, out
the gate, and was gone—lost in the street crowds—before
Ahab could recover enough to bellow, "Stop him!"

Elijah Told It Like It Was

The strangest part of this tale is—it *didn't* rain. At first no
one thought much about it. But as weeks, then months went
by without rain, people recalled the prophet's visit with
more respect. There wasn't even any dew to moisten the
earth. The trees and grass withered and died. Most of the
crops didn't even come up; those that had got started died
or bore no fruit. Well—next year. The people tightened
their belts. Next year would be better.

But the next year the ground was so hard a clod of it in
the hand could be crumbled into dry powder. It was useless
to plant seeds. You couldn't even get a plow in the ground.

The Bible says that the land was troubled and there was much suffering because of the drought. Jezebel ranted and raved and swore to kill every prophet of God in Israel. Ahab hunted for Elijah in vain. He had to be somewhere. But *where*?

The Man Who Came in from the Drought

Way back in the wilderness, far from any town or city, where the trees still gave shade and deep springs still fed little streams—was Elijah. He was there because that was where God had told him to go. And he was safe and sound, with shade and water—and *food*. Yes, food. For in that wilderness were wild ravens, wild *meat-eating* ravens. You guessed it. They caught small animals for their food, and they came to Elijah twice each day and left him his meals; he dined on things like choice roast rabbit and cold spring water. And there he lived, alone with God—until slowly the dryness crept even into the deep forests and the springs dried up and the brook he was camping by dried up. It was time to move on.

Marching Orders: Into Enemy Territory!

"And the word of the LORD came unto him, saying, Arise, get thee to Zarephath, which belongeth to Zidon, and dwell there: behold, I have commanded a widow woman there to sustain thee" (I Kings 17:8,9).

Zarephath? Good *grief!* Zarephath was a Phoenician city, not far from where Jezebel grew up! They were *her* people, they were Baal worshipers—and they had undoubtedly heard of Elijah's part in the famine. It was enough to strain anyone's faith. But Elijah's faith was simple and uncluttered. You could sum it up in four words: He just believed God. And he got himself up and went to Zarephath.

If God Says It, He Means It

It was a long hot journey, up the east side of the river Jordan, then far to the west. As far as he could see, the land was scorched and fruitless. Then at last, Zarephath, baked dry and overdone in the scorching sun. He stopped a moment, weary, and looked across the crusty sand toward the city. And as he looked he saw—yes, the figure of a woman. He started toward the city gate, and as he drew nearer he could see by her clothing that she was a widow. She was gathering sticks.

The Woman Who Went Out on a Limb

Elijah called out to the woman. "Bring me a little water in a vessel that I may drink." Water? Water was so scarce, she would have to be out of her mind to part with a precious drop! She started at first—and then, amazingly, she turned

to go through the gates to get it. He called out after her. "And bring me, I pray thee, a bit of bread also." Now asking for water was bad enough, but asking for *bread* was stark raving mad!

She stared at him a moment. "This is no ordinary man," she thought. And then—"Why, he is a man of God." Then she spoke aloud. "As surely as the Lord your God lives, I—I have no bread. I have a little—just a handful of flour in a jar —and a little oil in a jug. See? I'm gathering sticks to make a fire. I'm going—I *was* going to make a cake for myself and my son. After that—we'll starve. That's the truth, sire."

Elijah looked at her, thin, hungry, weathered by the sun. She had said, "The Lord your God." She was the one!

"Don't be afraid," he said. "Make me a cake and bring it to me. After that, make the cake for you and your son." There was silence. She looked at him—and straightened a little taller, waited.

"For the Lord God of Israel says the jar of flour shall not be empty and the jug of oil shall not run dry—until the day He sends rain upon the earth."

Now to say that this was a challenge is putting it mildly; actually this was monstrous! Asking her to give up the last bit of food she had for herself and her son? On a promise? But she looked at Elijah, and *she* decided to have the same uncluttered faith that he had—summed up in four words: She just believed God.

She hurried through the gates. Took her first great plunge in faith. Baked him a cake and brought it back. Then they went to her home. And there—yes, there was still flour in the jar and oil in the jug. She baked the cake for herself and her son.

The next morning there was *still* flour in the jar and oil in the jug. And all the mornings after that. Never much; always just enough. Just enough for that day.

Days of Waiting

Elijah stayed there with the widow and her son. And there he was safe. (God had sent him to the last place in the world anybody would think to look for him!) And he must have told her about God—how God had taken care of him, how He had known all about *her*. And had used her to be a part of the drama! She must have been amazed that God knew her *personally*. Why she was a nobody! This was wonderful!

The Little Faith that Almost Died

Now if your faith is a "sure thing," it's a sure thing that it will be tested. The widow's faith was tested, and in a most dramatic way.

One day her son fell ill. She did everything she could for him. But he grew worse. And worse. Until, before her horrified eyes, he stopped breathing. And her faith came all unpasted and fell in a million pieces at her feet. She turned to Elijah. "Why have you come here?" she wailed. Why, if *he* hadn't come, God would never have noticed her. "To remind me of my sins?" And if God hadn't noticed her, He would not be *punishing* her. "To kill my *son*?" What a jam she'd got herself into, baking this stranger a cake! Not very good thinking, but then her faith was new and fragile.

Elijah, bless his great heart, understood this. "Give me your son," he said softly, and he gathered the boy in his

arms and carried him up to his guest quarters on the roof of the house. There he stayed and there he prayed and begged God to bring the boy back to life again. "O Lord my God," he cried, "I pray you—let this child's soul come back into him." He looked down at the boy: the boy was breathing!

The Little Faith that Grew

How hopeless and frightened that widow must have been, waiting alone downstairs. How she must have run toward Elijah when he carried the boy back into the house. And how she must have *melted* with relief and gratitude when he put the boy in her arms and said, "Your son is alive." Her faith must have *soared*, for she said, "Now I *know* that you are a man of God. And that everything you told me about Him—is true!" And she must have felt a bit sheepish.

Operation Danger

By this time almost three years had gone by since Elijah had thundered at Ahab that dramatic day in the palace.

And now—and *now*—God said to Elijah, "Go show yourself to Ahab. I will bring rain upon the face of the earth." Go show himself to Ahab? Ahab and that wretched woman Jezebel? Go back to the roaring lions, and in their own den?

Precisely.

Elijah left the widow and her son. They waved good-bye until he was a tiny speck in the distance. Then he was gone. Gone back to finish the job he'd started—three years before. There was unbelievable adventure ahead. . . .

Think a Minute

The kingdom was a mess when Ahab inherited it. Do you think he might have been a better king? Who do you blame more, Ahab or Jezebel? Can you put your finger on the place where Ahab first went wrong? Where do you think Elijah's faith might have come unpasted? In front of Ahab? At the brook after it dried up? When the widow's son died? Which do you think was the hardest test? Do you think God would have been able to use the widow more effectively if she'd been rich or important or well-known? Does Elijah strike you as being almost too good to be true?

What About Today?

Can you think of times in your life when your faith almost came unpasted? Do you sometimes feel insignificant—sort of like a blob? Can you think of ways God can use you even though you might not feel very important? God arranged it for Elijah to find water, then to find the widow. Do you think He arranges your circumstances like that?

Does God REALLY Care?

One of the most important things for you to remember about God is that He *cares* for you. *Personally*. He has told you that even a sparrow can't fall without His notice, and that you surely are of more value than *many* sparrows. And that the very hairs of your head are numbered! (Matthew 10:29-31.) And He's told you to give Him your worries, your anxieties, your problems, for He cares for you affectionately and watchfully (Psalm 55:22 and I Peter 5:7). Try Him and see. He won't let you down. You can't lose for winning! Remember, He took care of the great prophet Elijah. But He also took care of the widow who was nobody.

How about memorizing this verse: "Therefore take no thought, saying, What shall we eat? or, What shall we drink? or, Wherewithal shall we be clothed? . . . for your heavenly Father knoweth that ye have need of all these things" (Matthew 6:31,32).

CHAPTER 6

The Greatest Showdown in History

Outside Ahab's palace, the lawns were scorched, the little pools dry, the gardens barren. Inside the flower urns and fruit bowls were empty. The desolation was now so great that even the royal family was feeling the pinch.

"We must do *something*," said Ahab.

"But sire, we've done everything possible—" began his advisors.

"I KNOW!" bellowed Ahab, and the flames in the braziers skittered backward.

They *had* tried everything. The search for Elijah was exhausted. The land was exhausted. The water was exhausted. And they were exhausted. Ahab turned to Obadiah, the governor of his palace. He knew Obadiah was a good and capable man. (What he didn't know was that Obadiah had been secretly hiding many of God's prophets in caves and sneaking them bread and water so Jezebel couldn't have them killed.) "Our most valuable chariot horses are in danger. And the donkeys for work," he said. "We must save the animals."

"Yes, sire," said Obadiah.

"Here is my plan," said Ahab. "We'll divide the land between us. And go search for shady places, for springs, for grass. We *can't* lose the animals."

"Yes sire," said Obadiah. And neither of them knew that they were about to run into the most hair-raising adventure of their lives.

Obadiah ran into it first. He ran into it while he was on his part of the search. It was a man coming toward him, and when he realized who it was, he fell on his face. "Elijah! Is it really you?"

"It is," said Elijah. "Go tell your king I am back."

"Go tell Ahab? And then have you disappear again?" wailed Obadiah. "He'll think I'm mad—he'll kill me! He's been searching for you! Didn't you hear that I saved a hundred prophets from death at Jezebel's hand? Why me? Do you want me to die?"

"As God lives," said Elijah, "I'll be here when he comes." And Obadiah went, trembling.

When Ahab was located and got the news, he hurried to meet Elijah, sputtering all the way. Now there'd be an end put to this nonsense. All his kingly bravado came back. When he finally met Elijah, he stalked up to him and cried, "Is that you, oh troubler of Israel?"

And Elijah descended upon him like a thunderbolt. "I have not troubled Israel! It is *you* who have troubled Israel —you and your house. You have turned away from God—to worship *idols!*"

Ahab stopped in his tracks.

"Now therefore—" Elijah went on—"*therefore*—gather all the people, and the prophets of Baal, and have them go to Mount Carmel. It is there that I shall answer your questions, King Ahab!"

So Ahab was the king. But Elijah was in authority. And the king obeyed the prophet!

The Contest Begins

What a picture it was! Mount Carmel, jutting into the Mediterranean Sea, with the dried-up river Kishon to the northeast and the scorched plains of Sharon stretching off to the south. And Elijah up there, and the people. Hordes of people, gathered and waiting. And the priests of Baal. And Ahab. Up in the HIGH place where the idols were worshiped, waiting for what was going to be the biggest showdown in history.

Elijah held up his hands for silence. And then he erupted like a volcano. "How long—" he roared—"how long will you go *limping* between two opinions?"

A shocked silence.

"If the Lord is God—*follow* Him."

Silence.

"And if Baal is God—follow *him!*"

Silence, though the people stirred uneasily.

"I, *only I,* am left as a prophet of God. There are 450 prophets of Baal—450 prophets—*of an idol!*"

No answer.

"Let two bulls be brought to us. Let the prophets of Baal cut up one, lay it on the wood, but make no fire. I will cut up the other and lay it on the wood, but make no fire."

There was a stir in the crowd, and a murmuring. "Then you call on the name of your god—and I will call on the name of the Lord. And the God who answers by sending down fire—"

The murmuring grew louder. "—He is *God!*"

The murmuring grew to a shout. They cried back that it was indeed a fair test.

Elijah turned to the prophets of Baal. "Choose one bull for yourselves, and prepare it first, for you are many. Then call upon the name of your god."

They began to prepare their bull.

"But put no fire under."

They laid the pieces on their altar. And the great contest began.

The Big Showdown

The prophets of Baal began to cry out to their god. Their cries were weird and terrible—"Hear us, oh Baal, hear us!" The morning wore on. "Hear us, oh Baal—hear us!" The heat began to come down, blistering the mountainside, and their bodies shone with sweat. "Hear us, oh Baal—*HEAR US!*"

At noon, Elijah began to mock them. "Cry louder!" he said. "For he is a god. Perhaps he's meditating, or perhaps he's busy."

Their cries grew into shrieks as they alternately leapt and limped around the altar.

"Perhaps he's gone on a journey and won't hear you at all—or perhaps he's asleep and needs to be awakened!"

They worked themselves up into a frenzy. They slashed themselves with knives so that the blood gushed forth—on, on, past noon—into the afternoon—under the merciless sun —Baal was the *god* of the sun—he must answer—he had to answer—Jezebel's god *had* to answer.

But there was no answer.

The afternoon wore on and they were fainting with weariness and there was no answer.

Then Elijah raised his arms again and beckoned to the people. "Draw near to me," he said. The crowd, weary, hot, stirred and drew nearer and watched him silently. He took 12 stones—twelve, the number of the twelve tribes of Israel —and repaired an old altar of the Lord that had been torn down. And then he did a strange thing. He dug a ditch around the altar.

Then he laid the wood in order on the altar and cut the bull in pieces and laid them on the wood. And then he said, "Fill four jars with water* and pour it on the offering. *And on the wood.*"

Wondering, they did as they were told.

"Do it a second time," he said.

They did, but now the crowd was murmuring again.

"Do it a third time."

This time the water ran off the altar and down the sides and filled the ditch and splashed and gurgled as they watched and listened, hearts beating fast now.

Then Elijah stepped up to the altar.

The sun was going down. It was the hour when, in far-away Jerusalem, the evening sacrifice was being offered in front of the Temple. The last rays of the setting sun reflected in his face, and there was a magnificence about him— and a great humility. His prayer was not frenzied as theirs had been. Or clever. Or brilliant. He just looked up into heaven—and talked to God.

"O Lord, God of Abraham, of Isaac, and of Israel—let it be known today that You are God—and that I am Your serv-

---

* They probably got the water from the Mediterranean.

ant—and that I have done all these things because You told me to."

The evening breeze had come up and it rippled his beard and his robe, as he stood there.

"Answer me, O God, answer me, that these people may *know that You are God*—and have turned their hearts back to You again—"

And then—

FIRE!

It rent the air with a great hissing and burst upon the altar with a great blinding light and it hissed and curled and licked at the altar until it had consumed the meat *and* the wet wood *and* the stones *and* the dust and *licked up the water that was in the trench!*

And the people fell on their faces and cried, "The Lord, He is God—the Lord, He is God!"

And Ahab watched helplessly, stunned and silent.

The Showdown Is Over/Or Is It?

Then everything began to happen at once. Elijah ordered the prophets of Baal seized—and taken down to the river Kishon—and killed. Then he turned to Ahab. Their eyes met—and Elijah knew what Ahab was thinking. "Go eat," he said, "for already I hear the sound of rain."

Ahab turned without a word and went down to his chariot to eat and drink. The people who were still milling around, rested, or ate their picnic lunches if they were fortunate enough to have them. Elijah went to the very top of Mount Carmel with his servant. And everybody waited. There wasn't a cloud in the sky.

Praying Can Be Lonely Business

Back up on the mountaintop, Elijah turned to his servant. "Go look toward the sea," he said quietly. The servant knew what he meant. Elijah knelt to pray, alone now. And he asked God for rain. The people had to know that the drought was because they had worshiped Baal. They had to know that God meant what He'd said. The rain had to come.

The servant came back. There was nothing. Elijah told him to go back—to go back seven times. And he kept on praying.

The servant went back, again and again, and again there was nothing. And then—

He came rushing back after the seventh time. There was a cloud rising up out of the sea—but only as big as a man's hand!

But Sometimes the Answers Are Spectacular!

Elijah got to his feet. "Go down and tell Ahab to hitch his chariot and get back to Jezreel, lest he get bogged down in the mud." *Mud?* Suddenly mud was a beautiful word.

Already the wind was blowing Elijah's hair and whipping his robe about him. Already the heavens were black with windswept clouds. Elijah started back down the mountain.

Farther down the mountain, the people milled about, excited, tense. Ahab and his party hurried to their chariots and he gave the order—"To Jezreel!" And he thought—"To Jezebel." And he was frightened. And then—

The rain! It came down in torrents! It whipped across the plain and danced on the hard earth and gleamed on the

59

rocks and came pouring down the mountainside in rivulets and then in streams! The children danced in it and splashed in it—people held their faces up to it and opened their mouths wide—folks who had never spoken to each other before, hugged each other for joy! It seemed as though the earth itself would cry out in thanksgiving and praise!

But the strangest sight of all was—Elijah! He had tucked his long robe up into his belt, and was running—RUN-NING—ahead of Ahab's chariot! And he ran—yes he *ran*—all the way, the whole twenty miles of it—to Jezreel!

For the *Spirit of the Lord*—was upon him!

What's It to You?

Maybe your life isn't as spectacular as this story—but can you think of times when God has answered your prayers—and in a quiet way it's been just as great?

And how about your choices? And how about your convictions? Memorize "How long halt ye between two opinions? if the LORD be God, follow him . . . for it is written, Thou shalt worship the Lord thy God, and him only shalt thou serve" (I Kings 18:21 and Matthew 4:10).

And think about it.

CHAPTER 7

The Prophet
Who Panicked

When Ahab got back to the palace, the courtyard was flooded and the rain was still coming down in great sheets, now silver in the moonlight. If he hadn't been a king he would have been asked to "wipe his feet." But kings do not have to "wipe their feet" as we ordinary people do. This, alas, was the only thing he had to be happy about.

He had to face Jezebel.

"You don't have to tell me it's raining," she said. "I know it's raining. What happened?"

He stared at her.

"Well?" she said.

He told her about Elijah's speech—"How long will you go limping between two opinions?" And "If the Lord is God —follow Him!" And "If Baal is God—follow *him!*" And then he told her about Elijah's instructions, about the fire, everything.

"Jezebel," he said at last. "It was Elijah's God who sent the fire."

"Elijah's God!"

"It was Elijah's God who sent the rain."

"Go on." Her face was a mask, waiting.

"Your prophets have been killed."

"My prophets killed? The prophets of Baal? They defied *Baal*? And you just stood there—"

"Yes, I just stood there," he said heavily.

They waited a moment, facing each other. Then—

"Send Elijah this message," she said. "Tell him—that as surely as his name is Elijah and my name is Jezebel, I'll have him killed by tomorrow at this time!" And she pulled a bell cord for a servant.

Guess Where?   Guess WHO?

A few days later, and eighty miles away in the wilderness, a man crouched in the shade under a juniper tree. He was a prophet. A few days before he had stood on the top of Mount Carmel and defied a king, a queen, and hundreds of false prophets. He had called down fire from heaven, and then rain. And then he had run twenty miles in triumph to Jezreel, ahead of the king's chariot. Elijah? No!

Elijah, yes.

When he had got Jezebel's message that she was going to have him killed, he had fled with his servant to Beersheba, which was about as far as he could go and still be in the original kingdom of Solomon—(look on your map!). And he'd left his servant in Beersheba and had gone a day's journey into the wilderness, alone. Fled at God's command, the way he had gone to the brook in the wilderness and then to Zarephath? No, fled for his life, in terror, and *not* at God's command. Elijah, scared?

64

Elijah, scared.

Elijah, scared and hungry and thirsty and utterly exhausted. Elijah, to put it bluntly, had had it.

"It's enough, Lord," he prayed there under the juniper tree. "I've had enough. I'm a miserable failure. Just let me die." And before his prayer was hardly over, he fell asleep from sheer exhaustion.

Now God could have said to Elijah, "Elijah," He could have said, "You are right. You *have* had it, and what's more, you *are* a miserable failure. You are, as you say, through. And *I* am through with *you*." But He did not. He knew Elijah was only human. And He knew exactly what Elijah needed. Rest. He let Elijah sleep and *sleep*.

God Is Merciful

A few hours later, someone touched Elijah on the shoulder. It was an angel of the Lord! "Arise and eat," the angel said. Elijah sat up. There, right at his head, was a cake baking on some hot stones, and a jug of cool water nearby. Suddenly the angel was gone. But the cake and the water were still there. Elijah ate and drank—and sank back and fell asleep again!

He slept, dreamless and deep, getting back his strength, and then someone touched him again. It was the angel. "Arise and eat, for the journey is too much for thee."

No question, no quibbling. Elijah did.

By now he was rested. And by now he should have most certainly come to his senses and done something right—but what? Gone back to Jezreel? Asked God what to do? *What?* Well, we don't know what he *should* have done; the Bible only tells us what he *did*. He got himself up and fled farther from Queen Jezebel, all the way to Mount Horeb (also called Mount Sinai; remember Mount Sinai—and Moses?) which was two hundred miles away in *Arabia*. And there he found a cave and there he *hid*.

Still scared.

It was there that the voice of the Lord came to him again.

God Is PATIENT

"What are you doing here, Elijah?"

Well, this was a stopper. What *was* he doing here? What indeed? In all his rational thinking he could not find one reason why he *was* here. He had gone berserk in the face of all of God's leading and he was *here* and he had to find some reasonable explanation for it. And he did what all of us do when we are backed into a corner. He tried to justify himself.

"Lord," he cried, "I've been doing my best for You—but the Israelites have forsaken You for other gods and they have thrown down Your altars and killed Your prophets and now I am the only one left who believes in You and now they are trying to kill *me!*"

This? From the prophet who had defied Ahab and Jezebel and all the prophets? *This?* This was, clearly, a cop-out. And God knew it.

God Is WISE

God knew it, and He also knew just how to deal with it. "Elijah," God said, "go out of your cave and stand on the mountain."

Well.

It must be said for Elijah, that although he had "copped out" temporarily, he still knew God was God. And out he went.

It came suddenly—a great wind, so great that the rocks were torn from the mountainside, sliding down and crashing about him and tumbling beneath him. He cringed into the mouth of the cave—

And waited. Surely God who sent down fire and rain on Mount Carmel would speak now out of the wind. But the voice of the Lord was *not* in the wind. Elijah waited.

And then—

The earth cringed beneath him and shook and quivered and rent and tore and shifted and gapped open and tore again and he hung onto the edge of the cave and shook with terror—an earthquake! Surely the God of the spectacular would speak out of the earthquake! But there was no voice. Elijah waited.

Then fire! Raging over the mountainside—leaping high into the air! Elijah shrank back into the cave. *Now* God would speak, out of the fire!

But there was no voice, nothing. Just a great silence. The forest was hushed—it seemed as if even the leaves stopped rustling and the birds stopped and listened. Everything seemed to be listening. Then, out of the silence, a still small voice. Elijah did not know whether he heard it or *felt* it. But he knew it was God.

Elijah covered his face with his mantle and went out and stood at the entrance to the cave. There it was again. "What are you doing here, Elijah?"

"The Israelites have forsaken You," Elijah began (and he

must have spoken softly now, too)—"and I, only I, am left —and they are seeking to kill me." And he proceeded to tell God all his troubles again, only this time he wasn't talking *at* God; he was talking *with* God, and now, at last, he was also willing to listen.

And he discovered that he had *not* failed. There was still much work for him to do. His marching orders are in the Bible.* And the exchange between them might have gone something like this:

"Go to Damascus—"

"Yes, Lord."

"And when you arrive, anoint Hazael to be king over Syria—" (Syria was not Israel's enemy at that time.)

"Yes, Lord."

"—and anoint Jehu to be king of Israel. And anoint Elisha to be a prophet, for in time he will succeed you."

"Yes, Lord."

"And Elijah—"

"Yes, Lord?"

"There are still seven thousand people in Israel who have not bowed down their knee to Baal."

"Oh." (sheepishly)

What a revelation *that* must have been! Elijah had not been alone after all. It was encouraging. And it was also embarrassing, in view of all the talking he had done.

Well, Elijah got himself up and did as he was told. Without being discouraged now, without running scared, and *without talking back*. He anointed the kings. And he anointed Elisha.

* I Kings 19:15-18.

A Young Man to Keep Your Eye On

He found Elisha in a most ordinary place, doing a most ordinary chore—plowing a field. He was following the oxen, holding the plow, marking the damp earth with clean deep furrows. Elijah took off his prophet's mantle, and walked over to Elisha, and without a word, threw the mantle over Elisha's shoulders—and walked away!

Elisha understood the sign at once. He let go of the plow and ran after Elijah and said, "Let me tell my father and mother good-bye—then I'll follow you."

"Go on back," said Elijah. "Settle it for yourself."

The choice was up to Elisha. And he made it. He said good-bye to his parents and followed Elijah. And jumped into history and into the most extraordinary adventures and—

But that's another story. Keep your eye on Elisha. In a few chapters, he'll turn up again. . . .

How About You?

How's *your* spiritual temperature? Depends on where you are? Depends on how you feel?

It shouldn't.

Sharon was absolutely "on fire for God" at camp. The messages, the buzz sessions, the campfire meetings, the testimonies—God spoke in such *spectacular* ways! But once back in school. Oh, good grief. Nobody in any of her classes was even a Christian. When somebody asked her what she'd done at camp, she could have invited the questioner to her Girls' Club at Church or told him *what* God *had* done at camp, or—

But she said, "Daaaaaaah"—and changed the subject. And at home, in the ordinary things, the chores, the humdrum, when God *wasn't* working in spectacular ways and she was tired—she pooped out. There *was* a twinge there, somewhere inside her, but just a *little* one—and she ignored it.

It was the still small voice.

The Holy SPIRIT?

Really? Yes, really. The Holy Spirit of God—He's the still small voice. Once you have accepted Christ as your Saviour, the Holy Spirit is sent to live in the very center of your personality (John 14:16 and I Corinthians 6:19). And He's going to give you twinges, whether you like it or not (and sometimes you won't). He does more than give you twinges, though. He will give you power (Acts 1:8). He will guide you (John 16:13). He will help you pray (Romans 8:26). And He will *assure* you that this is for real (Romans 8:16).

Right now, do you feel like "the prophet who panicked"? Forget it. God knows you have your ups and downs. Pick yourself up and go on!

And while you're picking yourself up, memorize this verse: "Howbeit when he, the Spirit of truth, is come, he will guide you into all truth: for he shall not speak of himself; but whatsoever he shall hear, that shall he speak: and he will show you things to come" (John 16:13).

How about *that?* You can't lose!

So get going!

CHAPTER 8

Haven't You Learned
Your Lesson <u>Yet</u>?

Who, Elijah?

No, Ahab.

And you guessed it, he hadn't.

While Elijah had been going about his business, Ahab had been going about *his*—and it could have been all good, but it turned out—

Well let's see what happened.

Three Messages—All Bad

Ahab was ruling his kingdom in peace. Elijah was out of the way, the ground was producing crops again, and as the wags would put it—Ahab never had it so good.

Until that message.

It was from the king of Syria, Ben-hadad by name, and it brought Ahab up with a jolt.

It seems that Ben-hadad had surrounded Samaria (the capital!) with a huge army and the message said: "Your silver and your gold are mine; your wives and your children, even the fairest, also are mine."*

It was very much like a ransom note; if Ahab gave over his wealth, Ben-hadad would go away in peace.

Problems!

And strange as it seems, Ahab, without a struggle and without hesitation, decided to pay the "ransom." He sent back word to this effect, and hoped that would be the end of the whole nasty business.

But it wasn't. Ben-hadad was bolder now; he wanted more. He sent back a second message saying he would send his army into Samaria and plunder and take away everything in sight! And then he settled down with his leaders and began to drink, while waiting for an answer.

When Ben-hadad's second message reached Ahab, he called his advisors. "Look what we have *now!*" he cried. "First he wanted my wealth and wives and children and I said yes—now he wants our total destruction!"

"Monstrous!" they thought, and "Don't do it!" they cried. And Ahab said to Ben-hadad's messengers, "Go tell your king I heard him the first time. To his *first* demand, the answer is still yes. To his second demand—emphatically *no.*"

Ben-hadad drank some more with his leaders while he mulled this over in his mind and then he sent back an angry reply. "There won't be enough *rubbish* left in Samaria for each of my people to get a handful!" he bellowed. If it were

* I Kings 20:3, Amplified.

74

in the language of a world leader in recent history, it would have said, "We'll *pulverize* you!"

"He's just putting his war gear on," Ahab shot back. "Tell him not to boast until the battle is over and he takes his war gear *off*."

When Ben-hadad heard this (as he was *still* drinking) he gave the order: "Set the army in array—get ready to fight."

You can see that Ahab was in a bit of a spot.

God Comes to Ahab's Rescue

What? God comes to *Ahab's* rescue? Yes, you are reading correctly and no, it is not a misprint.

A prophet *of God* came to Ahab with a message: "Thus says the Lord. Have you seen what a *multitude* Ben-hadad's army is? I am going to deliver it into your hands today; and you shall know that I am the Lord." And the prophet gave Ahab instructions as to how to lead his army.

Ahab was quick to follow the instructions; if this was going to be a victory, he was all for it. And if it was going to be a victory, it would have to be the Lord's—for Ahab's army was pitifully small and Ben-hadad's army was enormous!

The Battle that Went in All Directions

The battle started at noon. Ahab sent a small company of strong young guards out first. And Ben-hadad's spies reported to him, "There are some men coming from Samaria."

"Whether they've come for peace or war," said Ben-hadad, who was quite drunk by this time, "take them alive."

And that was the last order he gave that made any sense to anybody. For behind the small company of young guards, the Israelite army poured out of Samaria. And then—

Bedlam!

Ben-hadad and his captains were by now too drunk to command their soldiers properly and the result was chaos that finally turned into a rout! A "rout" is described in the dictionary as a disorderly flight, and that's exactly what it was. Ben-hadad barely escaped with his life, on a horse, with his cavalry—and the rest of his army? Practically *pulverized*.

The Lord's battle? Well, not according to Ahab. At least we don't have a clue in the Bible that he ever thanked God, or even admitted that God had a part in a *smidgen* of it.

Chances, Chances, How Many Do We GET?

You'll never believe it, but practically the same thing happened all over again. Yes. A prophet of the Lord came again to Ahab and told him to strengthen his army—Syria would attack again next year.

Sure enough. Old Ben-hadad was at it again. He and his leaders figured that "Israel's gods are gods of the hills; *that's* why they won. Let's fight them in the plains—and we'll have it made!" (It's the last thing they should have said; it was their undoing.)

This time the Syrians chose Aphek to attack. It was in the lowlands. *Now* they'd see!

Well, humanly speaking, it did look hopeless, absolutely hopeless. Here was the Syrian army, stretching back as far as you could see, until it seemed to fill the whole earth. And here was the Israelite army, so small it looked like a flock of lost baby goats.

Good grief.

BUT: A prophet of the Lord appeared *again* to Ahab, and said (and get this, it is very interesting), *"Because* the Syrians have said, The Lord is God of the hills, but He is *not* God of the valleys, therefore I will deliver all this great multitude into your hand, and you shall know and recognize *by experience* that *I am the Lord."**

Well!

It happened, of course. Complete chaos, followed by a rout, in all directions, and everywhere at once. The Syrian army was demolished. Ben-hadad was captured. All the cities that his *father* had captured were returned to Israel. Did Ahab thank God?

He did not.

"I Want What I Want When I Want It"

As the years went on, Ahab became more and more wrapped up in himself and he made, as the saying goes, a very small package. But in the business of the vineyard, he got about as small as he could get. The vineyard? Well, you'll find it's hard to believe but it went like this.

The vineyard was next to his palace in Jezreel. It struck Ahab one day—(when he was idling and had nothing better to do) that it would make a very nice herb garden. All he had to do was go make an offer to the owner, who was a

* I Kings 20:28, Amplified.

chap by the name of Naboth. Which he did.* But he ran into a snag before he even got started. "I can't sell it," said Naboth. "It's my inheritance from my fathers. And it has to stay in the family. It's our custom." Which should have been the end of it—a little property deal that didn't go through. But Ahab was not used to taking no for an answer.

Now it isn't polite to call a grown man a spoiled brat, but Ahab *did* act like one. He went back to his palace in a snit, threw himself on his bed, turned his face to the wall, and refused to eat.

When Jezebel heard of his tantrum (and that's what it was) she went to him and said, "What's wrong with you? I've seen you sulk before; what makes you so unhappy that you can't even *eat?*"

He told her about his problem for all the world as if it had been a big affair of state, of earthshaking importance.

And Jezebel bristled. *She* wasn't used to taking no for an answer either.

"Get up and eat," she said, "and let your heart be happy. *I'll* see that you get your vineyard."

Ahab did. And Jezebel did. And *what* she did can go down in history as an example of how small you can get.

How Small CAN You Get?

Jezebel wrote letters to the leaders in Jezreel with Ahab's seal on them. (And you can be sure that Ahab jolly well knew about it; she could never have used his seal without his knowledge.) And they said, in effect:

* I Kings 21:2, Amplified.

"A national calamity! Proclaim a day of fasting and sorrow—someone has said evil things about the God of Israel!" Jezebel worshiped Baal, but she had the mind of a Philadelphia lawyer. She knew what the penalty for saying evil things about God was. It was *death*, according to the Jewish law.

To Be Small You've Got to Be Sneaky

Small she was. And *sneaky* she was. And this is what she did. She uncovered two rascals who were willing to swear that *Naboth* (poor Naboth!) was the villain who had cursed God.

The rascals swore it. And the people believed it. And they *stoned Naboth to death*.

"I've Got What I Want—"

"Go take possession of your new vineyard," Jezebel said to Ahab. "Naboth is dead." And Ahab (who had been conveniently looking the other way while all this intrigue was going on) dashed off to Jezreel to inspect his prize. Yes indeed, there was no doubt about it, Jezebel was a very clever woman. The vineyard would make a splendid addition to the palace grounds. Nice piece of property—

And then he stopped in his tracks.

"—But the Price Is High"

There in the vineyard stood a man dressed in a coarse camel hair garment—a man whom he had not seen in six

years. The man he hated and feared more than anyone on earth.

Elijah!

Ahab knew he was in for trouble.

Great Is Our Lord

He knew that God who had sent the fire and the rain *was all powerful* (omnipotent). And God who had given him victory over the Syrians both in the hills and in the flatlands *was present everywhere* (omnipresent). And surely God who knew every nasty bit of mischief in Ahab's heart and who had sent Elijah here to find him *had unlimited knowledge* (omniscient). This was no God to *trifle* with!

"Have you found me, oh my enemy?" Ahab sputtered.

"Yes, I found you!" said Elijah, "because you have sold yourself to do evil in the sight of the Lord."

The Message

They squared away and stared at each other, there in the vineyard. "Lo, says the Lord," began Elijah, and Ahab knew it was going to be bad, all bad. And it was.

Ahab's family would be cut off from the throne of Israel. Jezebel would meet a violent death. And as for Ahab himself? Elijah had nothing to prophesy concerning Ahab personally, but the hint was there—a real strong hint. And it was simply: Watch it!

Ahab Decides He'd BETTER "Watch It!"

Ahab got the message. He tore his clothes. He put on sackcloth. He went on a fast. And for once in his life, there was no haughtiness, no stubbornness, no back talk. The Bible says he "went *softly*."

Well, it was about time.

What's It to You?

Write down something you want. What are your plans to get it? Any of them sneaky? How far are *you* willing to go to get your way? Don't you feel silly?

God is everywhere, knows everything and has unlimited power. This is one of the most magnificent verses you will ever learn: "Hast thou not *known*? hast thou not *heard*, that the everlasting God, the LORD, the Creator of the ends of the earth, fainteth not, neither is weary? there is *no searching* of his understanding" (Isaiah 40:28).

CHAPTER 9

The Last Hurrah

The last warning, in the vineyard, had left Ahab thoroughly cowed, and for three years he ruled his country quietly and in peace.

The Little Idea that Grew

But if there was any one thing Ahab had a peculiar talent for, it was forgetting about warnings. He could not seem to learn a lesson and make it stick. And so, after three years of "going softly," he was ripe for trouble again. It began with an idea in his mind, and a desire (mischief usually does). He'd been at peace, all right, but only because he couldn't afford a war; his army was too small. And there *was* one thing he wanted—a little matter with the Syrians he wanted to settle. To put it simply, the Syrians still had control of a walled city called Ramoth-gilead that really belonged to Israel. (Look on your map—it's way over, east of the Jordan.) And Ahab wanted it back.

Now when you have something brewing in your mind like that, the next step is an *opportunity* to help you put the wheels in motion. The opportunity came when the king of Judah paid Ahab a visit.

Hold On a Minute!

Jehoshaphat was his name, and he was a good king. His kingdom of Judah and Ahab's kingdom of Israel were friendly now, for Jehoshaphat's son had married Ahab's daughter. The visit was an occasion for celebration, and Ahab pulled out all the stops and made a great show of hospitality. And then he got to the point. "I want to get Ramoth-gilead back from the Syrians. Are you willing to go to battle with me?"

"I'm with you, Ahab," said Jehoshaphat. "My people are as your people, my horses as your horses. *But*—"

And the "but" was like a bombshell.

"—*But*. First, let's ask the Lord if He wants us to do this thing."

Now Ahab was not exactly used to asking the Lord's will on anything, but "yes," he said, and "of course," he agreed, and what's more, he did it in style.

The Council of "Yes" Men

What excitement! All the people, and Ahab's prophets—400 of them—gathered at the entrance of the city gates. With two thrones set up for Ahab and Jehoshaphat!

"Shall I go to battle against Ramoth-gilead?" Ahab asked his prophets. And they knew what he wanted to hear. "Go!"

they cried, "for the Lord will surely deliver it into your hands!"

This all seemed too easy. Jehoshaphat was not convinced. He turned to Ahab. "Isn't there another prophet of the *Lord* here we might ask?"

"There is one," muttered Ahab, "but I hate him. His name is Micaiah. And he never prophesies good for me, only evil!"

"Don't say that," said Jehoshaphat. And Ahab was forced to send for the one man who would speak the truth for God and not just tell him what he wanted to hear.

"Go get Micaiah," he said gloomily to his messengers. And they waited.

While they were waiting for Micaiah, the 400 prophets repeated their advice. One of them—a prophet by the name of Zedekiah—came up to the kings with a pair of iron horns he'd made, and cried out, "With these you shall push the Syrians until they are destroyed!" And all the prophets agreed, and the hubbub was terrific.

One Against 400

The messengers who went to get Micaiah told him, "All the prophets are telling the king what he wants to hear. Why don't you?"

And Micaiah said, "I'll say only what the Lord tells me to say."

When the messengers arrived with Micaiah, the great crowd separated to let them through. And Micaiah stood before the two kings. Everyone was quiet.

"Micaiah," said Ahab, "shall we go battle against Ramoth-gilead?"

87

"By all means," said Micaiah quickly, "for the Lord will deliver it into your hand." Everyone was astonished! Ahab stared at Micaiah. Was he mocking? He *had* to be!

Ahab was furious. "How many times do I have to warn you to tell me nothing but the *truth* in the name of the Lord?" he bellowed.

"You really want the truth?" said Micaiah. "Here, then, is the truth. I saw all Israel scattered upon the hills, like sheep without a shepherd; and the Lord said, 'These have no master. Let them return every man to his house.'"

Ahab sat staring. He knew what that meant. The master of the soldiers was himself—if the soldiers had no master and were scattered like sheep, it meant he was going to be killed in the battle—it meant Micaiah was prophesying his *death!*

He turned to Jehoshaphat. "Didn't I tell you he would say nothing good concerning me, but only evil?" And then to his servants, "Take this fellow to prison. Feed him on bread and water, until I return from battle—victorious!"

As they were leading him off, Micaiah said, "If you *do* return at all in peace, the Lord has not spoken by me." And then to the people, "Hear this, every one of you!"

And so they dragged him off.

But he had had the last word.

Ahab: Color Him Sneaky Again

The two kings went up to battle. Ahab was furious. He was also a little queasy. What if Micaiah were right? "I'm the one they'll be after," he said to Jehoshaphat. "I'm going to disguise myself as a common soldier; you dress in your royal robes. No one will know who I am—or where."

Now this little trick put poor Jehoshaphat in a bit of a spot. And why he agreed to do it is a mystery, but he did. And it nearly cost him his life.

The Trick that Didn't Work

The battle started. The armies met—and clashed—and the king of Syria gave the command—"Fight with neither small nor great, but find King Ahab of Israel and kill him!"

So naturally they looked for a chariot with a king in it, and naturally when they saw poor Jehoshaphat they surrounded him. And would have killed him on the spot, but he cried out—!

And they turned back just in time.

But where was *Ahab*?

The Last Hurrah

Where was Ahab indeed? In the thick of the battle, disguised in soldier's clothing. No one thought to chase him. Clever clever Ahab. His plan had worked. That stupid prophet would eat his words. Clever—UH!!!

Ahab slumped forward, an arrow sunk deep into his body, between the joints of his armor. An arrow shot at random, from the bow of an unknown soldier. "Take me out of the battle," he gasped, "I've been wounded." His driver looked at him in terror, then steered the horses through the dust, out of the path of battle.

They propped him up in the chariot, facing the Syrians, and the fighting raged on. And by nightfall, he was dead.

The battle was over.

And a great cry went throughout the army—"Every man to his city and his own house! The king is dead!"

And the soldiers, left without a king—scattered—and went to their homes—like sheep without a shepherd.

Just as Micaiah had said. Just as God had said. Ahab had been defying God all his life. This was the last time God tried to tell him what to do. And this was Ahab's last hurrah.

THE LORD HAD SPOKEN.

What's It to You?

Just that there's a limit to the number of choices you get! And Ahab's story is a horrible example.

"All scripture is given by inspiration of God, and is profitable for doctrine, for reproof, for correction, for instruction in righteousness" (II Timothy 3:16).

Are you listening?

The Battle
that Won Itself

Nobody Bats 1.000

But what about Jehoshaphat? He lost too. He lost the battle, along with Ahab—and he nearly lost his life! And he was, as we say, one of the "good guys"!

Well, he *was* a godly king. He'd done away with most of the idol-worship in his country. He'd strengthened his cities. He was held in high esteem by his own people—and the Philistines and Arabs too. *And*—he carried out a training program in what we'd call "Bible Study" for his people that was stupendous. He sent priests and teachers all over the country to teach his people about the Word of God!

But no one is ever so godly that he never makes a mistake. And Jehoshaphat was no exception. He'd let his son

---

Chapter 10 is also to be used with worksheet 9.

---

marry the daughter of Ahab and Jezebel, for one thing (enough said!). And now he'd gone up to battle with Ahab after God had said clearly that they should *not* go.

Takes a Big Person to Admit It

No, God did not let him get away with his mistakes. Jehoshaphat returned home from his escapade with Ahab, only to be met by a prophet who wrapped him smartly on the knuckles and told him God was displeased. "Should you have helped the ungodly King Ahab?" said the prophet, "and loved those who hate the Lord? And gone against His wishes?" Well there was only one answer to that one and Jehoshaphat knew it. He admitted he'd done wrong. And he asked God to forgive him. And God *did* forgive him. But He *didn't* take all his problems away.

This Problem Is Too Much!

Not one enemy attacking, but *three?* Yes, three! The armies of Ammon, Moab and Mount Seir—*all* threatening to invade Judah! When Jehoshaphat got the news, he issued orders so fast his leaders got stuck in doorways to carry them out. Declare a national fast! At once! Call everyone in Judah to Jerusalem! At once! A national calamity!

People poured into Jerusalem from every city. Everyone who could possibly come. Whole families. And Jehoshaphat faced the huge assembly.

And before them all, he prayed to God. "We have no might to stand against this great company that is coming against us. We do not know what to do—*but our eyes are upon You!*"

What? Do Nothing?

That's exactly what God said. He told Jehoshaphat to send his men to the cliff of Ziz. To fight the enemy? No—to *stand there*. Don't panic—just believe God! This time, when Jehoshaphat asked for instructions from God—he listened!

Thanks—for WHAT?

And all the people worshiped God and thanked Him for the strange instructions. And the next morning the army started out for the cliff of Ziz. "Believe God!" Jehoshaphat reminded them. And he appointed singers to march before them and sing praises to the Lord and give *thanks*. For *what?* Well they did not find out for what, until they had followed the instructions to the letter. Right up to the cliff of Ziz. And when they looked out over the plains—

The Problem Had Already Been Solved

The three armies lay strewn on the fields—everyone dead, to the last man!

What had happened? The armies of Ammon and Moab suspected that the army of Mount Seir would betray them. What to do? They decided to squash Mount Seir's army first. And in the confusion, even Ammon and Moab began to fight against each other until everyone was fighting everyone else! The result? Not a man left alive! God had won the battle for them before they ever reached the battlefield.

Jehoshaphat's men went into the fields and gathered the spoils ("loot," to you). Then they assembled in a valley and thanked God for the victory. Then they returned to Jerusa-lem, grateful and glad.

This time everyone had done everything *right*.

What's It to You?

Any character in Chapters 9 and 10 could be you. You could be like Ahab—not wanting to know what God wants you to do, and when somebody does tell you, having a trick or two up your sleeve to make it come out *your* way, or else. You could be like Jehoshaphat, wanting to know, and when somebody does tell you, going along with the gang anyhow. Or you could be like Jehoshaphat was the second time—wanting to know, and when somebody does tell you, *obeying*. Or you could be like Micaiah—standing up against the gang, come what may.

Who are you?

And what's your problem? Believe God—and obey. You might find He has already solved it for you!

CHAPTER 11

There's a Lot to See--If You Keep Your Head Up

Ahab was gone. He'd stepped out of the drama, a pathetic figure, squirming and rebelling to the last gasp. Now it was time for another character to go. But this character had streaked across the pages of history like a meteor, on fire for God all the way.

It was Elijah.

Who's Left to Do the Job?

What? Elijah going to leave? Who'd take over? And with what? Who else had the terrific power Elijah had?

Elisha?

This chapter is to be used with Lesson 10 worksheet also.

Ten Years of Apprenticeship

Elisha walked along the Jordan valley with Elijah. It had been ten years since that strange day when he'd been plowing in his father's field and that great prophet had come along and thrown that famous mantle over his shoulders.* Ten years since he'd decided to follow Elijah. And he'd been following the grand old thunderbolt ever since, refusing to leave his side.

Those years had been both wonderful and strange—but the last few days had been the strangest of all. For they had been visiting the various groups of young men—"sons of prophets"—Elijah had been teaching down through the years. And each group they'd visited, the young men had said to Elisha, "Do you know that the Lord is going to take your master away from you today?"

Elisha knew, but he didn't want to talk about it. "Hold your peace," he kept saying, "Yes, I know—hold your peace."

But now Elisha was mulling these things over in his mind. He turned and looked at his companion. By now they were at the edge of the Jordan River.

Big Shoes to Fill!

Elisha watched while Elijah took off his mantle. Would he put it over Elisha's shoulders again? Was this the time? But instead, the prophet rolled it up tight. And then he struck the water with it. And before their eyes, the water parted. And they walked across on dry land. And as they

* Chapter 7.

100

went, Elisha thought of the tremendous power God had given this great man. And he thought of himself. Would he be big enough to carry on?

Ask for ANYTHING?

When they got to the other side, Elijah stopped. And turned toward Elisha, "Ask what I shall do for you before I am taken from you."

Now Elisha could have said, "Give me more instruction," or "Give me some of your great brain," or "Give me a letter of recommendation so everyone will know that I am a great prophet." But he did not.

He knew that, more than he needed anything else, he needed God's power. "I pray you," he said, "let a *double portion* of your spirit be upon me." What he was saying was, "I want what you've got—and I want twice as much!"

Elijah looked at him for a moment. "You have asked a hard thing," he said. "However, if you see me when I am taken from you, it shall be so for you; but if not, it shall not be so."* And they walked on.

With God—Anything Can Happen!

What, exactly, did Elijah mean? Did he mean if Elisha saw him die? Did he mean—

Suddenly everything was fire! A chariot of fire! Horses—of fire! Coming between them even as they were talking! And then a great whirlwind—and Elijah and the fiery

* II Kings 2:10, Amplified.

chariot and the horses were swept up into the air! And Elisha cried out, "My father, my father! The chariot of Israel and its horsemen!" And then the chariot and the horses and Elijah were swept into the sky until they were out of sight!

And everything was quiet.

Elisha stood staring at the sky for a long time. And then he looked at the ground.

The mantle! Elijah's mantle! It was laying there, left behind. Laying at Elisha's feet.

He picked it up slowly. He walked back to the edge of the river. And, with trembling hands, he rolled it up tight. Then he cried out, "Where is the God of Elijah?" and he struck the water and—

The water parted!

And he started back across, on dry ground. The power of God that had been in Elijah was now in him.

A Man for All Seasons

When the young men Elijah had been teaching saw Elisha coming back from the Jordan alone, they said, "The spirit of God that was in Elijah rests on Elisha!"

It sure did. And everyone who crossed his path from then on, felt the power of it.

There Was This Humble Widow . . .

When she came to Elisha, she was in real trouble. No doubt about it. Her husband had been one of the prophets. Now he was dead, and she was in debt. Now in those days there were no loan companies and no credit cards and no welfare checks. When you got in trouble, you sweat it out. Her creditors were about to take her two sons as slaves, in payment of the debt. Seems harsh, but it was the custom of the times. There was no other way out. "What do you have in the house you could sell?" asked Elisha.

"Nothing," she said. "Oh yes—there *is* a pot of oil." But her face must have read negative, for oil was used for food, for lamps, for medicine. It was of great value to sell—but you couldn't do without it! To sell the last pot of oil in the house was sheer foolishness. Surely Elisha wouldn't expect her to do that!

He didn't. But he did ask her to do something that seemed as foolish.

"Go borrow containers from all your neighbors," he said. "Empty ones."

She looked at him. Empty containers? Whatever for?

"And not a few," he added. This was getting more improbable by the minute. "And when you've done this, shut your door on you and your sons. Then take your little pot of oil and pour it into all the containers."

Pour that little bit of oil into *all* the containers? She must have looked a little startled.

"Setting aside each container when it is full," he finished. This was unbelievable. What *was* Elisha up to?

The Pot that Poured as Much as It Could—

Whatever he was up to, it was worth a try. And the widow was not about to argue. She sent her sons scurrying to borrow empty containers from her neighbors. And when she felt she had enough, she closed the door on herself and her sons. The great test of faith was about to begin.

"Bring me a container," she said, and they did. She began to pour. They all watched. She poured from her little pot of oil. And poured. And poured. Until the big container was full. Now this of course was impossible; still it had happened before their eyes. There was a silence. Then, "Bring me another," she said, her faith stirring a bit, almost afraid to get carried away. They did. She began to pour again. The oil kept coming and *coming*—this was absolutely unreal! She set the container aside, and looked up, her face incredulous. "Another," she said. They did. And this time her faith *soared* as she poured the oil and poured the oil and poured the oil. "Another!" It still worked! "Another!" Again! "Another! Another—*what did you say?*"

"There are no more containers," said her sons.

"No more containers?"

"That's all we borrowed," they said lamely. She looked at them a minute, then tipped the little pot up a bit to see. Sure enough. The oil stopped pouring.

—And No More

She dashed back to Elisha to tell him how she'd filled the containers. "Go sell the oil," he said, "pay your debts and live on the rest of the money."

Wonderful!

She dashed back home to tell her sons. The oil was theirs, no strings attached. They talked excitedly together about it, thankful to God. Absolutely wonderful!

They had all the oil they wanted, all the oil the containers could hold, all the oil—

Wait a minute.

Why hadn't they borrowed more containers? Elisha had *said*, "Not a few."

Actually they had as much oil as they'd had faith. And not a drop more.

There Were Others

• There was this great lady. She gave Elisha a permanent guest room in her home. And through Elisha, God promised her a son. And when that son got sunstroke and died, she got upon a donkey and went after Elisha—

It's a cliff-hanger story.

• There were these students in Elisha's Bible class. And while they were having their seminar a servant gathered vegetables to prepare them soup. And he picked some poisonous gourds by mistake and when it was discovered—

• There were these other students, gathered to study with Elisha, and a few barley loaves and ears of corn were all they had to eat. But Elisha took them and—

You can find the endings of these accounts in II Kings,

Chapter 4. Story after story of people who crossed Elisha's path. And each one exciting. For people who crossed Elisha's path got their lives shaken up, whirled around, turned upside down—and usually sat down again, HARD. And they went away, never to be the same again. Because when people met Elisha, they met God.

What's It to You?

When people cross your path, do you think they go away better? Worse? Just the same? Can you think of times in your life when you might have got more from God if you'd had more faith? (Think of the widow.) Can you think of times when you were able to make a decision (a tough one) because God gave you the power? Elisha's power was not in himself. It was from God. So is yours.

"For I the LORD thy God will hold thy right hand, saying unto thee, Fear not; I will help thee" (Isaiah 41:13).

CHAPTER 12

Miracle by Long Distance

This is a story filled with enough intrigue and suspense and surprise twists to satisfy the most demanding adventure-lover. It's a story of VIPs,* and plenty of them, and yet in some strange way it is also a story of an ordinary girl. She's called a "little maid" in the Bible; actually she was probably just about the age of a sixth grader. She lived in Israel. That is, she started out living in Israel, but Syria (remember Syria, the old bugaboo enemy of Israel?) had a pesky habit of invading cities in Israel upon occasion, and it was during one of these skirmishes that she was carried off as a prisoner of war. So one minute she was a happy girl with nothing more to worry about than how to carry a jug of water on her head gracefully, and the next minute she was rounded up along with hundreds of other women and children and toted off to Syria as just part of the loot! To be made a slave!

*Very Important Persons

This chapter is to be used with worksheet Lesson 11.

Now to be a normal happy secure girl with a family one minute and then be just part of the loot the next is pretty humiliating business. And plenty to be bitter about.

The thing that makes this story so fascinating is that she *could* have been given to just anyone as a slave, but she was given to the household of the very man who had conquered her city!

His name was Naaman.

Who Naaman? Well Naaman was *the* most important general in the Syrian army. He was sort of four-star, you might say. You couldn't get to know him, or even get in to see him, if you were an ordinary person. You might write him a letter or ask for his autograph but that's about as far as you could get. But this girl got into his very household, and she was made a personal maid of his wife!

What a story to dream about and try to fill in the blank spaces! How it makes your imagination just go flying! What *about* this girl? She was probably *your* age. What did she do? How did she *feel?* Was she bitter? Let's take it as a story and read between the lines and see.

This Is the Time to Speak Your Mind

It was the beginning of a new life in a strange land for the little maid. The weeks rolled into months, and she found her new home not unpleasant—indeed her mistress was very kind to her—and they had many long talks together. She learned about Syria, and the strange gods they worshiped, and she told her mistress about the living God of Israel.

One day (and this is where the story begins) the girl was

attending her mistress. And from the window, she could see the general coming in the driveway in his chariot. He looked weary.

"Is that the general's chariot?" Her mistress looked weary too.

"Yes, mistress."

"He has been to the house of Rimmon with the king, to worship his god. It has done no good. I feel it."

"Rimmon?"

"The god of thunder. And lightning. And storms."

"What do you mean, it does no good?"

"Surely you know. You've heard the gossip. You know my husband has leprosy."

And *this* is where the plot thickens. For Naaman, with all his glory, with all his importance, with all his wealth, *had leprosy*—that most dreaded of all diseases. He was *finished*. And no god of Syria could help him.

"Yes, mistress," the girl said. "I know."

"You have tears in your eyes. Surely you cannot be sorry. You ought to hate us."

"You've been very kind to me. And God has kept me safe. No—I could never hate you."

"What a strange child you are. You speak of your God as if He were your father—"

"Oh, He *is!* He's a watchful all-powerful loving Father! I wish—"

"Yes?"

"I wish my lord the general were with the prophet in Samaria. *He* would cure him of his leprosy—"

"The prophet in Samaria?"

"Yes. Elisha. He is a prophet of God. God speaks to us through him. He—why he can do anything, practically. He just touched the river Jordan with his mantle and the waters parted and he walked across on dry land. He's brought people back to life from the dead! Once a poor widow had no money and he—"

"Do you think that he—this prophet—could cure my husband?"

"I know he could, my mistress. I *know* he could. Why once he—"

There was no stopping her.

This Is the Time to Make an Impression?

A few days later, Naaman set out for Samaria—but not for war. His caravan was packed to the hilt with lavish gifts —gold and silver and clothing. His soldiers and servants were dressed for company. And he had a letter from his *king,* no less, to the king of Israel! His wife had told him what the girl had said, he had told his king, his king had urged him to go and had given him a letter of introduction to be sure he got in at the top, with the best connections. After all, it's who you know that counts, and it was important to impress this God of Israel!

And so at last he was on his way. The girl undoubtedly watched him go. And thought, this was *her* doing—if the mission failed! She'd better pray.

This Is the Time to Hang On!

But from the beginning everything seemed to go wrong. Naaman got to Samaria safely, got his audience with the king, and gave him the letter. Everything was going very nicely. And then—

The king took the letter and read: "With this letter I send my servant Naaman that you may cure him of leprosy."

And he exploded.

Cure him of *leprosy*?

"Does he think I'm God?" he bellowed. "Does he think I can kill and make alive—sending me a man to cure of *leprosy*? He's trying to start something! He wants to create an incident! He wants to pick a fight!"

And he tore his clothes, and nearly declared all Israel a disaster area.

Things looked hopeless.

God Can Overrule the Biggest Bungler

But a young girl back in Syria had started all this and she had God on her side. So in spite of the bungling of Naaman and two kings, word did get to Elisha by the grapevine and he sent a message to the king: "Why are you so upset? Send him to me so he'll know there's a prophet of God in Israel."

The king did so. With vigor and ENTHUSIASM.

What's This?

Naaman drew up to Elisha's door with his chariots and servants and lavish gifts. He was anxious to see this prophet who worked magic. Undoubtedly he would come running out and put on one of his most impressive ceremonies—striking a pose, calling on his God, waving his hand over the sores—

But Elisha did not come out. Instead, a messenger came

out and said simply: "Go wash in the Jordan seven times and you shall be healed."

What? Preposterous! Wash in the *Jordan?* Was the prophet mocking? There were better rivers in Syria!

Naaman rode off in a rage.

Hopeless! Worse and worse!

This time, Naaman's *servants* saved the day. "Master," they said, "if the prophet had asked you to do some great thing, wouldn't you have done it? This is such a *simple* thing; *wash and be clean.*"

Naaman looked at them for a moment. Then, "Drive to the Jordan," he said at last.

Try God and See!

The water was dirty. The dipping was like a ceremonial washing, dipping the arms into the water, then raising them and letting it drip off the elbows. He had to wade in to his waist to do it properly and that was a pretty humiliating thing for him to do. He dipped and dipped. In front of his servants! More dipping. With all the clear rivers in Syria *and* Israel, Elisha had to pick this one. More dipping. Seven times.

He stopped and stared at where his sores had been. His skin was as pink and healthy as a baby's. There was not one sign of leprosy, not one.

At Last!

Could this thing be? What a proud and stubborn fool he'd been! He must go back and find that prophet; he must go back and find his God.

He did go back. Not the pompous windbag he'd been before. No. A humble man who'd come short of the glory of God. "Now I know there is no God in all the earth but in Israel," he said simply. Naaman had come home at last.

All the Way

Naaman went back to Syria on fire with his new found joy. He'd offered Elisha gifts, and to his amazement, Elisha had refused. There was nothing Naaman could do to buy what he had got from God—there was nothing he could do to impress God either. Amazing!

He not only had not left Elisha any gifts—he'd come away with something extra. Dirt! Dirt from Israel! Two donkeys loaded with it! So he could build an altar on it and worship Israel's God on Israel's soil. One thing can be said for Naaman, once he made up his mind, he made it up *all the way*.

How Do YOU Suppose It Ended?

And the girl? We don't know. We can only guess. But she *started* the whole business—it's hard to believe she wasn't in on the end of it. It's easy to imagine a conversation between her and her mistress. "You are an amazing child," the mistress says, "I cannot understand you. The general is cured—a whole household is turned upside down—it's all because of you, and yet your head is not turned."

"But I did nothing," says the girl.

"The prophet, then?"

"No. The God of Israel. Nobody else could do it. And even He would not have done it if—"

"If what?"

"If my lord the general had not dipped in the water."

"You mean the water cured him?"

"His obedience cured him. God cured him really. But he had to obey—*first*. He had to take Elisha's word for it that God was right—even if he didn't *want* to believe it."

You could go on and *on*. Did she lead her mistress to a belief in God? Did she—

What a story! How it makes your imagination *fly!*

What's It to You?

Who do you think you are the most like in this story? The "maid"? Are you concerned enough about others to tell them about God? Or do you identify with Naaman? Would you like to find God and don't know how?

It's simple obedience. The Bible tells us that "all have sinned, and come short of the glory of God" (Romans 3:23), and "the wages of sin is death" (Romans 6:23, and it means spiritual death, separation from God). What to do about it? Just believe what God said. "He so loved you that He gave His Son, that if you believe on Him you will NOT be separated from God but have everlasting life" (John 3:16, paraphrased).

Jesus died on the cross—for you. He was raised again— for you. "And many other signs truly did Jesus in the presence of his disciples, which are not written in this book: But these are written, that ye might believe that Jesus is the Christ, the Son of God; and that believing ye might have life through his name" (John 20:30,31).

CHAPTER 13

There's More Than One Way to "See"

The War that Went Askew

There was trouble ahead, trouble aplenty. The king of Syria decided to go a-warring against Israel. They'd been at peace for some time, but he was overripe for mischief again. And he was really quite sneaky about it. *Quite* sneaky.

He gathered his top-notch army commanders and they decided just where to attack. Then they chose a fine spot where they could camp and pick off the city they wanted to capture. It was all going to be so easy. Just camp in the right place and—POW!

They laid their sneaky plans carefully, and when they were ready, they marched in companies toward the chosen spot. Then they sent their scouts ahead to make sure the place was safe enough, and sure enough, POW!

This chapter is to be used with worksheet 12.

But the pow was not what they expected.

The spot was already occupied—the army of Israel was already encamped there! Armed to the teeth! Prepared to fight!

The Syrians were *not* prepared to fight. There was nothing to do but make a hasty retreat, which is a polite way of saying it was a "rout." What had *happened*?

The king called another conference of war. Was this a coincidence? Or was there dirty work afoot? Nobody knew for sure. There was nothing to do but plan another sneak attack —and hope it would work this time. They did. This time to another place the Israelites *surely* wouldn't suspect. They marched toward the place, sent their scouts ahead—

Oh *NO!*

The Israelite army was camped there, ready to go!

This was ridiculous! The king of Syria tried it again, this time tightening up his security and determining it would not happen again.

You guessed it. It did.

At the next conference of war, the king of Syria was tight-lipped and grim. "Tell me—" he roared—"which of you is a spy for the king of Israel!"

It was a tense moment. Treason was the worst crime imaginable for an army officer in time of war. When one of the officers finally spoke up, every other one held his breath. "Sire," he said, and everyone stiffened—"none of us is a traitor."

Silence. Then—"But Elisha, the prophet in Israel, could tell his king the words you speak even in the privacy of your own room here in Damascus!"

Of course.

That had to be it. Elisha knew where he planned to attack before he ever got there. Elisha knew because God was *telling* him. The only solution was to nab Elisha. *That* would do it. Very nicely.

Follow That Man

The scouts scurried about in Israel to find Elisha. And they did a good job. The report came back—Elisha was in Dothan, a city about eight hours' walking distance from Samaria. Well that made it all so simple. Just get Elisha and konk *him* out and all would be rosy.

The king of Syria gave his orders. Charioteers! Infantrymen! To Dothan, and seize Elisha! All these soldiers after one man? They couldn't lose!

They went on the prowl. Crossed the plain to the mountain where Dothan was located. They surrounded the city. Positioned themselves on the hillsides. Couldn't lose. The trap was set.

There's More to God's Power than Meets the Eye

In Dothan, high atop the mountain, Elisha's servant awoke the next morning. He yawned and stretched—and decided to go out and have an early morning look at the countryside. He looked and he saw—

Oh *NO!* The city was surrounded by an army—horses, chariots, officers, soldiers—the whole bit! They were done in!

He scurried back to Elisha. "We're done in!" he cried. And it sure looked as if they were. Done in.

"We're done in!" the servant was about to sputter. But

Elisha wasn't listening. Instead he raised his eyes to heaven and said, "O Lord—please open his eyes so that he may see."

See what? In the name of common sense, when they were all about to be captured—*what*?

And then the servant saw something—saw something—

Horses! Chariots! All of fire! It couldn't be! *BUT IT WAS!*

Horses and chariots of *fire?* Yes! *God* was with them!

The Trap that Sprang—on the People Who Set It!

Then Elisha did an incredible thing. He prayed again *that the Syrians would be unable to recognize him!* And then he calmly marched right up to the Syrian commander and said, "This is not the way—nor the city. Follow me, and I will take you to the man you are looking for."

Ridiculous? Ridiculous! But he did, and *they* did! They followed him and his men for hours, right—straight—into—

SAMARIA! Right into the very hands of the Israelite king and his forces.

Then he prayed: "LORD, open the eyes of these men, that they may see."* As calmly as you please!

And what's more, the Lord answered Elisha's prayer, and they *saw* where they were, and they were horrified. But when they *heard* what was being said, they were even *more* horrified. "Shall I kill them?" the king of Israel was saying.

They stood there, trembling. It had been like a nightmare. They couldn't believe it. They listened, frozen to a point. Every one of them. Their very lives were in the hands of this man of God. What would he *say*?

How Humiliated Can You Get?

And he said—"You shall not kill them. Would you kill captives you take in battle? No."

They listened, hardly daring to breathe.

Would he say torture them? Would he say—*what*?

"Prepare them a meal," Elisha said. Well that just about finished everybody off. Prepare them a *meal*?

That's what he said.

"Give them a meal so that they may eat and drink and return to their master."

This was unbelievable. And very humiliating. For if they ate, it was as much as promising the king their friendship forever. And if they *didn't* eat—

Good grief, they had no choice.

Very humiliating, very humiliating indeed.

So they ate.

* II Kings 6:20

123

A Peck of Problems—and God

And they went home defeated, and in absolute *disgrace.* Foiled, foiled, and *foiled.* And what had Elisha done? He had just believed God!

You've Got Problems?

Of course you have. What are they? Only you know. What do you do about them? You just believe God. And sometimes He tells you to just—stand—still—and *believe* Him.

What did David say? "Open thou mine eyes, that I may behold wondrous things out of thy law."*

And what does God say in I Samuel 14:6? "It may be that the LORD will work for us: for there is no restraint to the LORD to save by many or by few."

And how about memorizing Romans 8:35,37? "Who shall separate us from the love of Christ? shall tribulation, or distress, or persecution, or famine, or nakedness, or peril, or sword? Nay, in all these things we are more than conquerors through him that loved us." YET. Amid all these things we are MORE THAN CONQUERORS and gain an unsurpassable victory through Him who loved us.

You Shall Have Troubles

Sure. You sure will. God has never promised you *won't.* But He *has* promised to be there, every minute, to help you out of them—if you will only trust Him.

* Psalm 119:18.

CHAPTER 14

Sometimes You Have to Believe the Impossible

The Insoluble Problem

The city of Samaria sprawled on the slope in the hot desert sun. From the Shechem road a few miles away, it looked like a ghost town; there was no sign of life. Up closer, there were small stirrings of life, but they were only lepers outside the city gate. They rang their warning bells from force of habit, but they needn't have done so. The gates were heavily guarded. No one was going in or coming out. Samaria was under siege.

Years had gone by since God had given that spectacular victory—blinding the eyes of the Syrians so Elisha could lead them right into Samaria for total defeat-by-humiliation. Now Syria was waging an all-out, now-or-never, knock-down-drag-em-out war against Samaria and this time the king of Syria did not intend to lose. That monarch had pulled out all the stops, marshalled his entire army (not just

---

This chapter to be used with worksheet 13.

127

a few companies), completely surrounded Samaria, and dug in for a stay—a long stay. He had enough provisions to out-wait the people inside, no matter how brave they were. This time they would surrender or starve.

The Desperate Hope

Inside the city the people buckled down and prepared for the grim days ahead. The Syrian armies were all around them, shutting out all hope of food or help from the outside. The farmers could not go out to work their fields. No neighboring army could get in to help.

There was one thing in their favor—just one. They had Elisha. God had punished them before, but He had always come to their aid when the chips were down. Elisha was in the city!

The Awful Strain

Food was carefully rationed, food was hoarded, orders went forth from those in charge, to control the existing food supply. Then food rationing was tightened, food was stolen, food was the only topic of conversation. Then *anything* went, for food—anything. Horses, dogs, donkey heads. And anything went, to get it. It was a common thing now for people to kill—for food. They were crazed with hunger.

The Breaking Point

During these terrible days, the king made it a habit to walk on the city walls and look down into the streets—it was like inspecting a disaster area. Each time he did it, things were worse, and each time he did it, deliverance from God seemed less and less likely. Surely if God were going to come through He would have done so by now. It was true that Israel had always been an ungrateful and sinful nation, and God must be weary with them—but He'd always helped them before.

Why hadn't Elisha intervened? Why wasn't he *doing* something?

The king looked down at the streets in despair. His people were quarreling over food—they had become like *beasts!*

Why was Elisha so *silent?*

"Help us my lord, O King!" wailed a woman up at him.

"If the Lord doesn't help you, how can *I* help you?" he thundered back. What else could he say? He knew that he and all of Israel had sinned. But *somebody* had to be blamed. Somebody had to be the scapegoat. And then he tore his clothes, and in a fit of desperation cried out, "God do so and more also to me, if the head of Elisha stays on him this day!"

So Elisha was the scapegoat. It had come to this.

Nobody, even the king, could *think* straight anymore. The breaking point had come.

The Awakening

In another part of the city, Elisha sat in his house with his elders. It was obvious that the very days were numbered for most of the people in the city.

"My very *minutes* are numbered," said Elisha, "for already there's a messenger of the king on the way to remove my head. No—" he went on quickly as they started up in horror—"it won't be necessary to hide me. Just close the door against him. That will delay him long enough. For the king is not far behind him."

"The *king?*"

"Yes. And I have a word for him—from God."

And even as he spoke, there was a commotion at the door. The messenger was delayed a moment and, sure enough, as Elisha had said, the king and some of his officers were not far behind.

A very quiet king came into the room. All the anger had gone out of him. "This is from the Lord," he said. "This is punishment." They looked at each other for a moment. He went on. "And I can't wait any longer, expecting him to withdraw it. What, Elisha, *what* can be done now?"

The Promise

Elisha came right to the point. And it was a bomb-shell. "Hear ye the word of the Lord; Thus saith the LORD, Tomorrow about this time shall a measure of fine flour be sold for a shekel, and two measures of barley for a shekel, in the gate of Samaria."* They stared back at him. If he'd told them he was made of gingerbread they couldn't have been more astounded.

"Do you hear what the man says? He has gone mad!" It was the king's captain. "And how is all this going to come about? If the Lord made windows in heaven and poured down the grain upon us—*then* your prediction might come true!"

* II Kings 7:1.

130

"You shall see it with your own eyes," Elisha said quietly to the captain. They were all silent.

"But you shall not eat any of it," he finished. No one dared answer him. They turned on their heels and left.

It was twilight.

Meanwhile, Outside the Gate

Outside the city gate the twilight settled down like a living thing, filled with hopelessness and terror. Four lepers prepared to make their pitiful camp for the night. They moved slowly, listlessly. It was a dreary business. And hopeless. And then—

Suddenly out of the blue, the same thought came to all of them. And they all began talking at once.

"Why do we stay here until we die?"

"Are you thinking what I'm thinking?"

"We were mad not to think of it before. We can go to the Syrians."

"They'll kill us."

"So they might kill us. And so we'll die. It's what we're going to do anyway."

"I think we've gone mad with hunger. But they *might* feed us—and the worst they can do is kill us."

"Right!" they all agreed. And they staggered, helping each other, across no-man's-land, toward the Syrian camp.

Into the Jaws of the Lion

It was dark now. They talked in whispers. "This is where the guards should be. Just up there."

"Hold on to your bells. Keep them silent."

"The night watch might be—"

They stopped in their tracks.

"Wait a minute—there are no guards here."

The whispers grew louder as they scattered and started toward the camp.

"Strange—it almost looks as if—"

"There's nobody about, anywhere!"

"Are you sure?"

The whispers grew louder as they called to each other.

"Sure! Look! In here! And here! These tents are empty!"

"Clothing. And weapons. And food—"

"Food! Food over here!"

"And over here! Food over here!"

"We must have gone mad!"

"No! The camp is deserted!"

The Army that Wasn't There

They were right. The camp *was* deserted. For the Syrians had been snugly encamped one minute, and the next—

Out of the blue had come the thundering sounds of chariots and horses charging forward. An attack! AN AT-TACK! And the terrified Syrians had cried, "The king of Israel! He has hired the Hittites and Egyptians to come and wipe us out!"

And they'd fled in terror without even attempting to make a stand and fight back.

But it wasn't the Hittites. Or the Egyptians. The thundering noise they'd heard was not for real. God had affected their hearing just as He had affected the sight of the other army in the last chapter. They'd just *thought* they heard it!

The News Nobody Believed

The four lepers were in a flurry of excitement amidst horses, donkeys, tents, gold, silver, treasures, clothing—and FOOD! The food was all they could think of at first. Then they turned to the treasure. Grunting and tugging, they hauled off all they could carry into the darkness and hid it. Clothing, gold, silver, shields, spears, treasures—

And then they stopped in their tracks, conscience aprickling. "This is not right," they cried. "Here is this great news and we're keeping it to ourselves. We must go back and tell the king."

"Let's wait till morning."

"No! If we wait till then we might be punished. We must do it now."

So back they went, to the guards at the gate, who called out to messengers, who dashed to the palace. And told the king.

He couldn't believe it. "It's an ambush!" he cried. "They've gone off to hide knowing we are hungry. And when we rush out to camp we'll fall into their trap—they'll come back and kill us all! There's nothing we can do. Noth—"

But wait. There *was* something they could do. One of his advisors thought of it. And it was worth a try. "Send five charioteers out to investigate. If they are killed we lose nothing but five men and five horses, who would have died here soon anyway."

Made sense. They decided to try it.

It Was True!

A few hours later the city of Samaria was in an uproar! The five spies had gone out, and came back and reported. By daylight they had seen where the Syrian army had fled. And all the way to the Jordan River they had found clothing, shields, spears, treasures—that the frantic soldiers had dropped in their fright as they heard the thunder of chariots —the chariots that weren't there!

Overseers were appointed to keep order. And over them all, the king put in charge the very captain who had laughed at Elisha, to have charge of the city gate. And the order went out and the gate was opened—

Food at Last!

The cry that went up from Samaria that day was terrible to hear. And the struggling and the crushing and the panic in Samaria was terrible to see. The starving people descended upon the Syrian camp like locusts, and stripped it bare.

And as they poured back into the city with the loot—the place inside the gates was like a tremendous whirlpool of people—some pouring back in—some trying to get out—some waiting, begging—hysterical, reaching out with their hands—and their cry was like one great cry wrung out of hunger—

FOOD!

There was another cry of anguish but no one heard it. The captain who had laughed at God's promise went down under that avalanche of hungry people, and they trampled upon him and he was killed, and no one heard him cry out.

What God Says, He Means

And later, when the overseers had most of the loot in the storehouses and order was restored and things were properly organized, the shouts went through the city—"Two measures of barley for a shekel, and a measure of fine flour for a shekel!" But the captain who laughed at God was not there to hear.

And food was plentiful but he was not there to eat it. For Elisha had said, "Behold, you shall see it with your eyes, but you shall not eat thereof."

A sad thing. A sad thing indeed.

Sound Familiar?

It was the same story all over again. God had taken care of His people in great trouble, the way He *always* had. Some had believed Him. Some had not. Some had given up hope. Some had not. Same old story.

He had used His omnipotence* to create the miracle of the noise of the chariots. But He had used four ordinary insignificant men to tell the good news of that power. Four *lepers*.

What's It to You?

Are you like any of these people? Elisha, who never stopped believing? The king who doubted? The captain who laughed after he heard God's promise? The lepers, who stumbled upon the reality of God's promise, and decided to take their lives in their hands and go back and share it?

Which one could you have been? And which one would you be like now if you were in great trouble? Is there ever really any doubt that God is able to deliver us out of trouble?

Think about the memory verse for today: "Behold, the LORD'S hand is not shortened, that it cannot save; neither his ear heavy, that it cannot hear: But your iniquities have separated between you and your God, and your sins have hid his face from you, that he will not hear" (Isaiah 59:1,2).

Think About the Whole Book

What about it? Sure it's a story of a kingdom that fell apart. But it's a story of people too. For the story of kingdoms is the story of people, the story of the human heart, the story of—YOU.

What—*you*?

Yes—*you*.

* Infinite power.

You in trouble, you rebelling, you sorry, you doing right and you doing wrong. And the story of God with you, every minute!

One of the greatest verses in the Bible is directed right at *you*. "Who then can ever keep Christ's love from us? When we have trouble or calamity, when we are hunted down or destroyed, is it because He doesn't love us anymore? And if we are hungry, or penniless, or in danger, or threatened with death, has God deserted us? For I am convinced," St. Paul says, "that nothing can ever separate us from His love. Death can't, and life can't. The angels won't, and all the powers of hell itself cannot keep God's love away. Our fears for today, our worries for tomorrow, or where we are—high above the sky, or in the deepest ocean—nothing will ever be able to separate us from the love of God demonstrated by our Lord Jesus Christ when He died for us."*

For when you put your life in God's hands, things get worked out for you, sometimes in ways you least expect. And *the strangest things happen* . . .

* From Romans 8:35-39.